MAN AND THE WORLD

INTERNATIONAL LAW AT WORK

by Richard Deming

WILDSIDE PRESS

For Patty

Contents

MAN AND THE WORLD

Preface

This is the third and final book of a series designed to explain in lay terms how our legal system functions. The previous books were *Man and Society: Criminal Law at Work* and *Man Against Man: Civil Law at Work*. Except for some historical material on the development of law, both books were devoted mainly to law in the United States. While by its very nature this book has to range beyond that restricted point of view, the stress, insofar as possible, will be how international law affects the United States.

In both previous books it was pointed out that no one has ever succeeded in adequately defining the word *law,* despite the world's greatest legal minds bending their talents to the task. As a random example, the famous English jurist William Blackstone was quoted in the second book as defining a law as "a rule of civil conduct prescribed by the supreme power in a state, commanding what is right and prohibiting what is wrong." This seems a nice clear definition until you try defining "right" and "wrong."

It is not a great deal easier to define the three subdivisions of the law into which this trilogy is divided. However, some definitions are necessary simply to distinguish among the three. In *Man and Society* criminal law was defined as "that branch of the law which defines crimes and fixes penalties for them"; a crime was defined as "a voluntary violation of a law enacted to invoke the responsibility of individuals to the community, and therefore is an act injurious to the public. It may be an act of either commission or omission. That is, it may be a positive act, such as theft, or a negative act, such as failure to file an income-tax return."

In *Man Against Man* civil law was defined as "that branch of the law which regulates the legal responsibilities of persons to each other in their private capacities and resolves disputes between them. The term *persons* in this definition includes not only individuals but also partnerships, corporations, nonprofit organizations of all types, the various levels of government, the branches of such levels of government, or any other entity capable of bringing or defending a court action."

Although neither definition is perfect, each is a reasonable description of its respective branch of the law.

Like the word *law* itself, the term *international law* has never been adequately defined. One reason for this is that international law is constantly changing. For instance, the widely accepted definition prior to World War I was formulated about 1905 by Lassa Francis Lawrence Oppenheim, a German-born jurist who·became a noted professor of international law at the London School of Economics. He wrote: "International law is a body of customary and conventional rules which are considered legally binding by civilized states in their intercourse with each other." Changing times have almost totally invalidated this once authoritative definition. International law now consists of much more than "customary and conventional rules." Furthermore, it no longer regulates relations only between states, but certain international organizations, and even privately owned companies in some cases, have come to have at least limited rights and duties under international law.

The student of modern international law can find a variety of more up-to-date definitions that have superseded Oppenheim's, most of them tending to be rather long and involved. The author's own definition is:

International law is a body of principles, customs, and rules which are recognized as effectively binding obligations by sovereign nations and other international entities, and which govern the mutual relations between na-

tions, between nations and international organizations, between different international organizations, and between nations or international organizations and privately owed companies under certain limited circumstances.

Again this is no perfect definition, but it pretty well describes what international law is and does in the modern world. Political change, such as the eventual creation of a world federation of nations, for instance, may make it as obsolete in another generation as Professor Oppenheim's 1905 definition is today.

You will note that in the above definition the term *nations* was used in lieu of the more common textbook term: *states.* Wherever possible this will be the usage throughout the book, simply because the fifty political subdivisions of our nation are called states, and it is less confusing to restrict the usage of that term to them. There will be some unavoidable uses of *state* as a synonym for *nation* when direct quotes are given, however.

In international law the term *municipal law* has nothing to do with cities, but is the commonly used term for the domestic or internal law of a nation. That usage is employed throughout the book.

Because international law is such a vast subject, it was necessary to restrict the subject matter covered. Some specialized subjects such as diplomatic recognition, acquisition of citizenship, the status of stateless persons, the relations of privately owned companies to foreign nations, and the nationalization of industries have, because of lack of space, been either ignored or only briefly touched upon. The intent has been merely to explain what international law is and how it functions, rather than to write a comprehensive treatise on all phases of the subject.

Law being a subject that engenders strong personal opinions from all writers, some of the author's opinions are expressed in this book, as they were in the previous two. I wish to extend my thanks to UCLA Law School senior Connie Ferris for checking the script for technical errors and errors in terminology. She should not be held

accountable for any of the opinions expressed, as her
help was limited to pointing out inaccuracies. All opinions expressed are strictly those of the author.

—R.D.

Chapter I

THE ORIGINS AND DEVELOPMENT OF INTERNATIONAL LAW

Throughout recorded history some form of international law has developed whenever independent political units came into peaceful contact with each other. There is even some evidence that what might be called intertribal law developed in primitive societies when different tribes had such contact.

When the first Europeans arrived in North America, they found that among the Indian nations there was an elaborate set of rules and customs governing relations between them. Treaties and alliances were common, and there were fixed customs and ceremonies for the meeting of representatives to arrange such treaties and alliances —the passing of the calumet, or peace pipe, for example.

In South America anthropologists have unearthed a legend among the Warrau Indians that their conquest and subjugation by the Caribs, thousands of years ago, stemmed from a violation of intertribal law, the slaying of a child emissary sent to the Warraus on a peaceful mission by the Caribs. Actually, according to the legend, the act was a reprisal for the Caribs having slain a Warrau emissary, but there was a special taboo against slaying a *child* emissary (which may have been the reason the Caribs dispatched a child to represent them after their own breach of intertribal custom).

Intertribal rules and customs among primitive peoples were based on oral agreement, of course, for the simple reason that they had no written language. The earliest example of a *written* agreement between independent political units dates back to about 3100 B.C. Signed by the respective rulers of Lagash and Umma, neighboring

divisions of ancient Mesopotamia, it provided for arbitration of a boundary dispute and pledged to abide by
the ruling of the arbitrator.

There are only a few scattered written treaties extant
from the period of the next thousand years, probably
because most have simply been lost to history than because few were executed. But from about 2000 B.C. on,
many have survived in numerous parts of the world. Either the actual treaties themselves or accounts of them
indicate that even then agreements were common in
such diverse places as India, China, Babylonia, and
among the Hebrew nations on such matters as alliances,
the creation of vassal nations, extradition of criminals,
and the treatment of ambassadors.

As a random example, in 1272 B.C. King Ramses II,
of Egypt, signed a mutual defense pact with "the great
Chief of the Hittites" (who later became his father-in-
law) that, except for a clause binding both parties to the
agreement "forever," reads much like such treaties in
force today.

In the two previous books of this series it was shown
that the development of both criminal law and civil law
could be traced back to similar early origins. But no
such clear-cut development from the early international
relationships described above to modern international
law can be shown. As a matter of fact, most scholars
conclude that what few similarities there are between
ancient rules and principles of international cooperation
and modern international law are largely coincidental.
The world situation was so totally different in those ancient times from what it is today that the whole concept
of what international law is and what it should accomplish has changed.

In those early times the modern concept of a community of nations interdependent on each other for economic reasons was totally lacking. Nations were largely
self-sufficient, and contacts with other nations, either
peaceable or hostile, were largely limited to bordering
nations or those relatively nearby. At the time Ramses
II negotiated his mutual defense pact with the King of
the Hittites, for instance, both China and India had rela-

tively advanced systems of international law for dealing with the independent political units within their own spheres of influence. But it is extremely doubtful that Ramses was aware even of the existence of those two lands.

In other words, instead of the present global system of international law that has general acceptance throughout the world, there existed merely a number of regional systems with no interrelationship.

The origins of modern international law go back no further than about four hundred years, and lie in Europe. This was when nations first began to accept that certain international problems were global in scope instead of merely regional. While some scholars speak of the influence of ancient Greece and of the Roman Empire on the development of international law, actually neither had much impact on *modern* international law.

The bond of unity among the independent city-nations of Greece is sometimes pointed to as international cooperation at its best. But again this was a strictly regional arrangement, and there was no recognition by the Greeks of any rules of conduct for foreign relations outside the narrow confines of the Hellenic world. All nations outside of that world was lumped together as "barbarians."

Some writers point to the Roman Empire's *jus gentium* (the law of aliens) as a contribution to international law. But while that phrase was indeed an important one in the development of international law, it underwent two distinct changes of meaning during the centuries following its invention by the Romans. Originally, while *jus gentium* concerned foreigners, it was not international law, but merely a part of Roman municipal law.

In Rome *jus civile,* or civil law, applied to citizens only. When Rome, as the world center of trade, began to attract alien businessmen from all over the world, something had to be done to protect their legal interests. Because Roman citizenship was a jealously guarded privilege, the government was unwilling to allow it to lose any of its importance by extending to noncitizens any of its prerogatives, and therefore refused access by aliens to the regular courts. (Aliens were not necessarily from outside the Roman Empire. Many were from lands that had been conquered by Rome, but absorption into the Roman Empire did not confer citizenship upon the inhabitants of a conquered nation.) It wanted their trade, however, so about 240 B.C. it compromised by creating special magistrates titled *praetores peregrini* to apply *jus gentium* in cases involving *peregrini* (friendly aliens, as distinguished from *hostes,* or enemy aliens).

Originally *jus gentium* was supposed to be the law of the land of the alien involved in the action, or if two aliens of different nations were involved, a combination of the law of both lands. However, because magistrates were often unfamiliar with the alien law, they eventually came to apply the principle of *aequitas,* which simply meant "reasonableness." The word *equity* in our modern civil law derives from *aequitas.*

Jus gentium of the Roman Empire was therefore more of a contribution to our modern courts of equity than to international law. As a matter of fact, Rome made very little contribution to the development of international law. Most of its contacts with foreign nations were in wars of conquest. At the height of its glory it had subjugated all of the known world except the "barbarian" lands on the perimeter of the empire, and had no formal foreign relations with the barbarians.

During the Middle Ages the term *jus gentium* underwent its first change in meaning, when it came to be used by legal scholars to refer to the existence of a universal law among all nations. The theory was that the common elements of all legal systems (such as the universal law against murder) constituted a special universal system of law based on reason and unrestricted by national boundaries. Still this was in the category of municipal law rather than international law, because it concerned laws as they affected *individuals,* not as they affected nations.

During the Renaissance the term took still another meaning, and *jus gentium* came to mean a body of principles and rules that were assumed to exist between independent nations—not necessarily by formal agreement, but in many cases merely by tacit acceptance or through custom (e.g., respect for a flag of truce)—which governed the relations between such nations. In 1758 a Swiss writer on international law named Emmerich von Vattel translated the term as "law of nations" instead of "law of aliens." In 1780 English writer Jeremy Bentham slightly changed Vattel's translation, and it became "international law."

Thus, while the term from which "international law" derives traces directly back to the Roman Empire, the meaning of *jus gentium* had changed so much by the time it became "international law" that Rome deserves credit only for coining the term and not for giving birth to international law.

At this point it is appropriate to define another legal theory known as *jus naturale,* or natural law, that was in vogue during the same period that *jus gentium* began to develop its third meaning. The principle of *jus naturale* as it pertained to municipal law went clear back to the Stoic school of philosophy in ancient Greece. It had been refined and elaborated on in the first century B.C., however, by one of Rome's greatest scholars, Marcus Tullius Cicero.

Somewhat oversimplified, the concept of *jus naturale* is that all law has perpetually existed in nature, whether ever enacted or not. Therefore it is possible for judges to "discover" an appropriate law to cover any situation where no formal statute applies. The concept as defined by Cicero applied only to municipal law, but when legal scholars began to turn their attention to international law, it was inevitable that some of them should apply the principle of *jus naturale* to it also.

The origins of modern international law can be found in the sixteenth century, when European writers began to turn their attention to the subject. Writers throughout history had been expounding on the subject, but now an entirely new factor was introduced by a major change in world conditions. Plato, for instance, had proposed "ideal" rules for the relations between nations. The difference was that up until the sixteenth century rulers had piously agreed to the moral principles laid down by philosophers such as Plato, but seldom made any attempt to practice them. But now rulers and their ministers of foreign affairs, in Europe at least, actually began to give respectful attention to scholars writing on the subject, and to let such writings influence at least some of their relations with other nations.

This was primarily because the interrelationship of nations was changing so rapidly that a whole new set of rules was necessary. The New World had been opened to exploration and colonization, and European merchant vessels were also sailing to such far-off places as South Africa and the Far East. Instead of nations having only regional contact, the ships of nations that were geographically located far apart were now encountering each other on the high seas and in distant ports. New territories, far from Europe, were being claimed as possessions. While there was an arrogant tendency to consider the new international law as applying only to European nations, and to regard the new lands opening up as exploitable territories whose native inhabitants had only limited rights, if any, under the new law, contacts between representatives of different European nations were becoming common in remote parts of the world. Inevitably disputes arose over some of the contacts— such as squabbles over newly claimed territories—which required settlement.

Rulers and their ministers consequently turned to the scholar-writers who were beginning to write on the subject for answers to some of the perplexing questions arising from this rapidly increasing international contact all over the world. One of the earliest writers of importance was a Spanish professor of theology at the University of Salamanca named Francisco de Vitoria (1480–1546). In 1532 he published *The Law of War Made by the Spaniards on the Barbarians,* in which he attempted to define in theological terms what constituted a "just war." (The concept of "just war" as opposed to "immoral war" had been the subject of considerable ecclesiastical debate during the Middle Ages, without the matter ever being clearly resolved. At one point the Vatican decreed that under certain circumstances it was possible for both warring parties to have God on their side.)

Vitoria's work was largely an attempt to justify the Spanish conquest of the Aztec Empire of Mexico by Hernando Cortes in 1519 to 1521, but he also outlined a set of general rules for all warfare that was quite advanced for the time. Because it was a cruel age, his rules seem pretty barbarous by present-day standards, though. For example, he had no argument with the ancient principle that "to the victor belongs the spoils," and therefore found no moral fault in the looting of conquered cities. He did, however, condemn such purely vindictive practices as the deliberate burning of cities after conquest when no military advantage was involved, the torture of prisoners except to gain information, and the execution of prisoners without trial.

Francisco Suárez (1548–1617), a Spanish professor of theology at the University of Coimbra, published *Treatise on Laws and God as Legislator* in 1612. It was in this treatise that *jus gentium* was first given the third meaning mentioned earlier. Suárez was also the first to advance the concept that while nations were sovereign, they were *bound* by the rules of international law and not merely party to them when it was to their advantage.

Contemporary with Francisco Suárez ·was Regius Professor of Civil Law at Oxford University, Albericus Gentilis (1552–1608). Gentilis was an Italian Protestant who fled to England to escape religious persecution. In 1598 he published *Three Books on the Law of War*. In 1613, after his death, his *Pleas of a Spanish Advocate* was published. The latter was primarily concerned with the law of the sea, covering such matters as sovereignty over coastal waters, piracy, and the doctrine of freedom of the seas.

Gentilis's main contribution to the subject of international law was that to a large extent he succeeded in divorcing it from religion. Possibly through fear of being branded a heretic, he made no attempt at complete separation, but most of his arguments were based on past law and history rather than on the Bible and Church

pronouncements. This was a major departure from the
practice of previous and contemporary writers in the
fields of both municipal and international law.

Huig Cornets de Groot (1583–1645), more commonly known as Hugo Grotius, is generally considered
the father of international law. Grotius was born in Delft
and was educated in law at the University of Leiden,
where his father was curator. A child prodigy, he was
writing learned treatises by the age of fifteen. When only
twenty, he was commissioned by the States-General of
Holland to write a history of the Dutch, a project he
worked at on and off for the rest of his life and which
was not published until twelve years after his death.

In 1601, during the Dutch war of independence
against Spain, the Dutch East India Company captured
a Portuguese ship that was brought to Holland to be
sold as a prize of war. (Since Portugal was under Spanish control, Portuguese ships were classified as enemy
ships by the Dutch.)

To the astonishment of the Dutch Government, the
Spanish Government, and the board of directors of the
Dutch East India Company, some stockholders of the
latter protested the transaction, despite its potential for
high profit, on moral and theological grounds. After a
couple of years of legal wrangling, the company engaged
the young lawyer Hugo Grotius to write a legal opinion
on the matter.

Grotius completed *Commentary on the Law of Prize
and Booty* in 1604. As this was a commissioned report
to a client, the Dutch East India Company, and not a
book designed for publication, it remained in the company files and was not discovered by scholars until 260
years later. However, one chapter was excerpted and
published by Grotius in 1609 under the title *Mare Liberum* (The Freedom of the Seas).

While this treatise was a landmark in the history of
international law, it illustrates the difficulty even the
most scholarly writers on the subject have in being totally
objective by divorcing themselves from the interests of
their own nations. At the time Grotius published *Mare
Liberum,* Holland was a naval power. England, at that

time navally inferior to Holland, refused to accept the premise of freedom of the seas, holding to the position that when a nation controlled a specific section of the high seas, that made it a closed sea. But when England's navy began to grow, England reversed position and embraced Grotius's premise.

The Dutch East India Company commission sparked in the young lawyer a lifelong interest in international law. His greatest work, *Three Books on the Law of War and Peace,* was published in 1625 in France, where he was then living. In 1619 he had become involved with a group of religious dissenters popularly called Arminians, after the name of their leader, Jacobus Arminius, although they themselves rejected the title and claimed to still be members of the Reformed Church who merely differed in opinion on points of doctrine. Even minor religious dissent could bring swift and drastic action in those days, though. Despite being the chief magistrate of Rotterdam, Grotius was tried for heresy and was condemned to life imprisonment. Two years later he escaped and fled to France.

Three Books on the Law of War and Peace is regarded by some scholars as a cornerstone as important to modern international law as the Magna Charta is to English law or the Constitution to United States law. It was the first attempt to codify international law into a comprehensive catalog of rules to cover every conceivable type of international contact.

Despite its title, the work, like all previous works on the subject, dealt mostly with the law of war. Only a portion of Book Two was devoted to the law of peace. Grotius gave it more complete coverage than anyone before him, however, and the nineteen chapters devoted to peaceful contact between nations contain elaborate rules of conduct derived from classical writings, history, and the Bible.

Grotius wrote that there were two distinct types of law applying to nations. *Jus gentium,* or *jus voluntarium* (voluntary law), as he also called it, was law deliberately created by men *without* divine guidance—a theory that caused the Catholic Church to place his works off limits for Catholic readers. But there was also *jus natu-rale,* or natural law.

Voluntary law was not deemed by Grotius to be near-ly as important as natural law, but the mere fact that he made a distinction between the two types of law inevita-bly stirred controversy among subsequent writers. As a direct result three distinct schools of thought developed during the seventeenth and eighteenth centuries.

The Positivists taught that law among nations was created by men through treaties and accepted customs and that it was based on mutual agreement between na-tions. That is, there were no international laws that ap-plied to nations without their consent. Actually some members of this school conceded that there might be some natural law, but deemed it of only minor impor-tance if it existed. Richard Zouche (1590–1661), an Oxford professor, founded the school, but Cornelius van Bynkershoek (1673–1743), President of the Supreme Court of Holland, was probably the most important Pos-itivist writer. His most important works were *Dominion of the Seas,* published in 1702, *Jurisdiction over Am-bassadors,* published in 1721, and *Questions of Public Law,* published in 1737.

The Naturalist school of thought was founded by Samuel von Pufendorf (1632–1694), a professor of in-ternational law at the University of Heidelberg and also at the University of Lund in Sweden. In 1672 he pub-lished *Eight Books on the Law of Nature and of Na-tions.* While Pufendorf recognized the existence of treat-ies and international customs created by men of their own volition (their existence could hardly be ignored), he denied that they had the binding force of law. Only natural law, rather than the consent of nations, was binding, and its principles were binding on all nations regardless of whether or not they had agreed in advance to abide by them. He went to some pains to describe just what natural law was and how it could be "discovered." In essence he taught that natural law consisted of those standards of behavior that had been demonstrated through historical experience and logical reason to be essential to the good of man and to the good of human society in accordance with the design of nature. The "discovery" of specific law to apply to an international dispute therefore lay in the study of historical precedent, combined with reasoning out what nature would require in this particular instance to preserve peace and harmony.

Members of the third school of thought called themselves the Grotians. They held that both natural law and voluntary law were equally important and equally binding. In this they gave much more stress to voluntary law than Grotius himself had.

Most of the leading writers during the seventeenth and eighteenth centuries were of this school. Perhaps the greatest exponent of the Grotian school was a writer who has already been mentioned, Emmerich von Vattel (1714–1767), a Swiss diplomat. His major work was *International Law: or Principles of Natural Law Applied to the Conduct and Affairs of Nations and of Sovereigns,* published in 1758. For many years this book was accepted by European statesmen as the standard authority on international law and custom and was even frequently cited in decisions involving international law by the United States Supreme Court. It was referred to by that body in one decision as late as 1887.

Up through the period of the Napoleonic Wars these writers on international law were, for all practical purposes, the creators of what international law there was. Their works were consulted constantly by statesmen, and their opinions were cited by opposing negotiators in disputes between nations. But after the downfall of Napoleon I, an event occurred that changed the whole direction of international law. That was the Congress of Vienna, which met from September, 1814, until June, 1815, with a brief interruption after the escape of Napoleon from Elba and the resumption of the war until his final defeat at Waterloo on June 18, 1815.

The purpose of the Congress of Vienna was to discuss the European situation after Napoleon's defeat, and it was the most brilliant assemblage of monarchs and diplomats ever gathered together in the history of Europe up to that time. Every European power except Turkey was represented. Among heads of state attending were Czar Alexander I, of Russia, the Emperor of Austria, the Kings of Prussia, Denmark, Bavaria, and Würt- temburg, and numerous princes of smaller nations. Some of the most famous diplomats in European history were there, several of such stature that their names are still familiar to the average schoolchild. Among them were Prince Metternich, of Austria, Prince Talleyrand, of France, and England's Duke of Wellington.

The main business of the Congress of Vienna was to strip France of all the territory Napoleon had added to it by conquest and redistribute the territory in a manner designed to produce a "balance of power." That is, an attempt was made to rearrange Europe in such manner that no one nation, or probable alliance of nations, could become powerful enough to risk a war of aggres- sion against any other nation or alliance. To that effect Russia, Prussia, England, and a few other nations re- ceived new territories; other nations, such as Austria, had lost territory returned; and some new nations were formed. In the latter category Holland and Belgium were united into a single kingdom in order to provide a stronger buffer state north of France, and Norway and Sweden were joined.

The immediate effect of the congress was to create a balance of power that succeeded in maintaining peace in Europe for the next forty years. Its long-range effects were considerably more important, though. Almost as an aside from the main business, the congress took up some questions of international law that had nothing to do with the Napoleonic Wars. At the instigation of En- gland, for example it took the noteworthy step of con- demning slave trade as illegal under international law. It also provided for freedom of transportation along rivers that flowed across more than one nation or served as boundaries between nations. Such provisions as these, considered minor at the time in relation to such impor- tant matters as the creation of new nations, were in the long run the more important actions of the congress. The new nations formed have long since separated into their original states, but the precedent established of nations gathering together in congress to discuss and agree on principles of international law lives on.

The Congress of Vienna was the first time in history that world powers, along with their less powerful allies, met together and specifically agreed to abide by certain rules of international law in their future relations. It paved the way for numerous similar get-togethers since, with increasingly wide representation.

One of the most important such conferences, from the standpoint of its impact on modern international law, took place in Switzerland at the time the Civil War was going on in the United States. It is of sufficient·importance to merit an examination of the historic events that brought it about.

On June 24, 1859, during the war between Austria and the alliance of France and Sardinia, one of the bloodiest battles in history up to that time took place at Solferino, in East Lombardy, Italy. When it was over, forty thousand men lay dead or wounded on the battlefield.

A thirty-one-year-old Swiss banker named Jean Henri Dunant happened to be traveling on business in the area and arrived at the battle field just after the battle. He was so appalled by the lack of medical attention being received by the wounded and dying that he wrote a book, published in 1862, titled *Un Souvenir de Solferino* (A Memory of Solferino), in which he described the terrible carnage of the battlefield and suggested the establishment of relief societies to help the wounded of future battles. The book so gripped the public imagination of all Europe that there was widespread clamor to keep his suggestion alive.

Gustave Moynier, president of the Geneva Public Welfare Society, was so impressed by Dunant's book that in February, 1863, he formed a Committee of Five in Geneva to study the proposal and put it into effect. He appointed Dunant and himself as two of the five.

Considering that the five men were all private citizens of a relatively small country—Switzerland—and that the committee had no official status even in the Swiss Government, their success in imposing their theories on an international basis was phenomenal. Of course they had the advantage that at the Congress of Vienna Switzerland had been declared a neutral country without alliance to any other country, so that all nations were willing to listen to them at least. In any event, in October, 1863, the committee held a conference in Geneva to which sixteen different nations sent delegates. At this conference it was agreed that each country would establish a private society to work as an auxiliary of the army medical service to help treat battlefield casualties.

These persons, and all others whose duties were to help the wounded, were to be regarded as neutrals. In order to assure their protection, and also to assure the protection of hospitals and ambulances, a red cross was adopted as the distinctive emblem to be displayed. Thus was born the International Committee of the Red Cross (ICRC) and the first national Red Cross societies chartered by that organization.

The agreements made at this 1863 conference were merely in the nature of affirmations of principle and, as no treaties were signed, did not actually bind any of the attending nations to anything. But in August, 1864, a second conference was held at Geneva, again attended by sixteen nations, at which the famous Geneva Convention was framed.

Although the same number of nations attended this conference as attended the previous year, in some cases they were different nations. A notable addition was the United States, whose representative was Charles Bowles, of the American Sanitary Commission, the agency that ran Union hospitals during the Civil War. Mr. Bowles was there only as an observer, however, with no authority to commit his government to any agreement. It was another seventeen years before the United States became a signatory to the Geneva Convention.

The 1864 treaty concerned itself solely with the treatment to be accorded the wounded during wartime and the observance of the neutrality of the Red Cross symbol. But this was only the first of a series of similar agreements, all resulting from diplomatic conferences instigated by the Geneva Committee, each one attended by an increasing number of nations, which eventually resulted in a whole new set of rules governing the conduct of nations during wartime.

Up until 1949 none of these conferences resulted in new treaties, but only in revisions of and additions to the original one signed in 1864, so that clear up through World War II the set of agreements continued to be known simply as the Geneva Convention. In 1949 the term became plural when four separate conventions were signed. Most nations of the world are now signatories of the Geneva Conventions.

The original Committee of Five in the meantime not only had changed its name to the International Committee of the Red Cross but had grown in size. It is now restricted to a maximum of twenty-five members. It still remains a private, independent, and neutral organization composed exclusively of Swiss nationals, however.

While the ICRC charters national Red Cross societies, such as the American National Red Cross, it is not in any sense the international headquarters of these societies, although it does set certain rules and standards in granting charters. These societies cooperate on an international basis through an organization called the League of Red Cross Societies, also headquartered in Geneva. The main function of the ICRC is simply to make sure that the Geneva Conventions work.

In order to enable it to perform that function, the signatories to the Geneva Conventions have accepted the ICRC as a neutral agency with certain specified international inspection privileges. In time of war, civil war, or internal disturbance, the committee acts as intermediary between the parties opposing each other. Delegates of the ICRC are permitted to visit prisoner-of-war camps and civilian internment camps to inspect conditions and make sure health standards and the treatment of prisoners conform to the rules of the Geneva Conventions. Delegates also work for the repatriation of the wounded and the return of unwounded prisoners to their own countries. They distribute emergency relief in areas devastated by conflict, attempt to reunite separated families, and assist the war-disabled. The ICRC also acts as a central clearinghouse for prisoner-of-war information sent to it by all belligerents, arranges for mail between prisoners and their families, and traces missing persons.

In all these functions it deals impartially with all belligerents without taking sides and without making judgments as to who is in the right or in the wrong.

Three factors have tended to shape the course of international law since the Congress of Vienna. The first has been an increased willingness on the part of nations to submit to rules of law, a matter that will be discussed in more detail in Chapter III. The second has been the signing of an increasing number of conventions to which an increasing number of nations are party. The third has been a changing philosophical approach to international law on the part of most governments.

The first such change in philosophical approach was the rise of the Positivist school of thought to predominance over both the Naturalists and the Grotians. By the end of the nineteenth century the theory of natural law was being mentioned by scholars only as a historical curiosity (although it still has some advocacy among Catholic scholars insofar as ecclesiastical law in concerned). By 1900 most authorities on international law recognized only the voluntary agreement between nations as the source of international law.

During the latter part of the nineteenth century and up until World War I the Positivist point of view was reinforced by the widely accepted theory of "absolute sovereignty" of nations. Under this theory each nation was a law unto itself and was accountable to no other nation or to the world for either its internal or external actions, providing the latter violated no formal agreement. In short, no action by a nation, including military aggression, was illegal under international law unless the nation concerned had specifically committed itself by treaty not to perform such an action.

Unfortunately this was not merely a textbook theory, but the principle of absolute sovereignty was accepted by most heads of state and by most diplomats. The result was an era of "power politics" during which the militarily powerful nations expanded both their territories and their economic influence at the expense of weaker nations. Germany's demand for "a place in the sun" in the early part of the twentieth century was merely its way of expressing its determination to get its share of the spoils by employing the same kind of power politics the world's larger nations had been using for a couple of generations. But like the robber barons of industry who flourished about the same time and were beginning to demand laws to protect their immorally gained wealth by banning the very practices they had used to accumulate it, the "have" nations had no desire to give up to any upstart nations some of the gains power politics had brought them. The inevitable result was World War I.

Since the end of World War I, and accelerating after World War II, there has been a steadily changing outlook among both scholars of international law and statesmen. More and more it has become generally accepted that nations have moral responsibility for their actions that reach beyond mere treaty obligations. The strongest indication of this has been the passage of a number of resolutions by the United Nations Security Council formally condemning certain actions by nations as morally reprehensible (such as the April, 1973, condemnation of Israeli attacks on Lebanon).

The present tendency is to regard international law as being based largely on treaties and custom, but to concede that nations also have moral responsibility in their dealings with other nations. There is a growing trend among international arbitrators and jurists to feel that when no rule based on treaty or custom is available to point the way to a proper recommendation or decision, such recommendation or decision should be based simply on the principle of justice.

Some see this as an approach to international law rather similar to the old Grotian philosophy of two types of law, voluntary and natural, one based on agreement between nations, the other on abstract principles of moral law.

News reports of a new war breaking out somewhere in the world as soon as the last one has ended may make it seem that international law has dismally failed to pre-

vent war from continuing to be a major method of settling international disputes. But despite armed conflict
somewhere being an almost constant condition, the em-
phasis of international law during the past century has
changed from setting rules for warfare to concern for
peace. The latest Mideast conflict, set off by the Arab
attack on Israel during the latter's 1973 celebration of
Yom Kippur, illustrates this in dramatic fashion. Obviously international law failed to prevent the war from
starting, but it effectively halted it. If the basic philosophy of the major powers remained the same today as it
was a hundred years ago, it is probable that the United
States would have intervened on the side of Israel and
the Soviet Union would have stepped in to help the
Arab states, with the probable eventual result of the two
superpowers being drawn into war with each other. Instead both worked for peace, and the machinery of the
United Nations Security Council brought it about.

Chapter II

HOW INTERNATIONAL LAW IS MADE

The only source of municipal law in *civil-law* countries is legislation, whereas there are two sources in *common-law* countries: legislation and judicial interpretation.

Civil-law countries (which include most of continental Europe) have codified systems of law. That is, all laws have been systematically arranged into a comprehensive code that is applied by the courts as the sole basis of judicial decision. While previous court decisions may be taken into consideration by judges, if they so desire, such previous decisions are not binding, because precedents do not make law under codified systems as they do in common-law countries.

Common-law countries, which include both the United States and England, have systems of law, in general force throughout their nations, based not only on statute but also on custom and usage.

In the United States legislative bodies on all levels of government—national, state, and local—are constantly passing new laws and revising or repealing old ones. But the process of lawmaking does not stop with legislative action. Eventually every law must be tested in court, and judges make law by their judicial interpretation.

Courts may void laws on various grounds—most commonly because they violate either the state or the federal Constitution. This as effectively repeals laws as though they were repealed by legislative action. Similarly court decisions can make positive law. The 1963 Supreme Court decision in *Gideon v. Wainwright,* which required indigent persons accused of serious crimes to be furnished lawyers at public expense unless such service was deliberately and consciously waived, is an example of judicial lawmaking. It made brand-new law in the thirteen states that up until then had made no provision for such service.

In civil cases, but never in criminal cases, judges in the United States sometimes render decisions based upon common law, where there is no specific legislation governing the matter before the court. Common law may be defined as custom so widespread and so generally accepted that it has the force of law. It applies only to civil law in this country because only violations of specific statutes are grounds for criminal prosecution. In a sense, therefore, common law can be regarded as a third source of municipal law, although it would probably be more accurate to describe it as merely a resource for judicial opinion.

The sources of international law are in some ways similar to the sources of municipal law in the United states, in other ways quite different.

The greatest difference is that the *prime* source of municipal law in the United States—and in all nations, for that matter, whether common-law or civil-law countries—is legislation, and *no* international law stems from that source. The Security Council and the General Assembly of the United Nations bear some resemblance in organization to the Senate and House of Representatives of the United States Congress, but their functions are quite different. The United Nations is in no sense an international legislature and has no power to pass laws binding upon the member nations. Nor had the defunct League of Nations before it. Municipal law is binding upon all persons under its jurisdiction, regardless of whether they agree with it or not. No citizen of New York State, for instance, can declare that he is not subject to a law passed by the state legislature because he did not give his formal approval to its enactment. On the other hand, while some rules of international law are considered binding even upon nations that have not formally agreed to them, most international law relies on voluntary agreement between nations.

One of the organs of the United Nations (the United

Nations as a whole will be discussed in detail farther on) is the International Court of Justice. Since this is the highest court of international law, the sources of international law it looks to in ajudicating disputes should be pretty good evidence of what those sources are. Article 38(1) of the Statute of the International Court of Justice says:

> The Court, whose function is to decide in accordance with international law such disputes as are submitted to it, shall apply:
> (a) International conventions, whether general or particular, establishing rules expressly recognized by the contesting states.
> (b) International custom, as evidence of a general practice accepted as law.
> (c) The general principles of law recognized by civilized nations.
> (d) . . . judicial decisions and the teachings of the most highly qualified publicists of the various nations, as subsidiary means for the determination of rules of law.

Some authorities object to the limitations of this list, but before we touch on possible sources these critics would like to see added, we will discuss the four sources listed in Article 38(1).

TREATIES

The term "international conventions" in clause (a) means treaties. In international law the word "convention" always means a treaty and is never used as a synonym for a meeting or for custom and usage. Actually its usage in clause (a) is a bit unfortunate, because the term is most commonly used to describe multilateral treaties, such as the Geneva Conventions, to which all nations are invited to become signatories and which lay down general rules of international law by which the signatories agree to abide. By using the phraseology "international conventions, whether general or particular," the clause includes both multilateral and bilateral treaties (treaties between only two parties), but the terminology is awkward.

Treaties come under many different names. In addition to *convention,* some of these names are *agreement, protocol, statute, convenant, engagement, accord, provision, regulation, arrangement, declaration, act, charter,* and *pact.* Some of these words have meanings in international law in addition to meaning *treaty,* however, which creates something of a problem in terminology. Also some of the terms refer to specific types of treaties and therefore are not precise synonyms for the general term *treaty.* For purposes of simplification the term *treaty* will be used in this study unless either a more precise term is needed to indicate the nature of an agreement or a specific agreement is cited that has an identifying name using another term—the Warsaw Pact, for example.

A treaty is a contract between two or more nations or international organizations. In general there are two types of treaties: lawmaking treaties and contract treaties.

A lawmaking treaty is one that binds the signatories to certain courses of action under specific circumstances. The signers of the Geneva Conventions, for instance, have agreed to rules of conduct in the event of war, such as the humane treatment of prisoners. The treaty has thus made positive international law.

A contract treaty is merely a business agreement. The much publicized wheat-sale agreement of July 8, 1972, was a contract treaty. It merely provided for the sale of a large amount of grain to Russia by the United States at a price favorable to the Russians. Our government has been party to hundreds of such contract treaties in the past without exciting more than passing interest from the public, but this one happened to make the front pages because of charges that advance information of the pending deal was improperly leaked to certain American businessmen by government officials, resulting in some exorbitant profits at the expense of the American taxpayers.

The difference between the two types of treaties is only in their contents, and often there are multiclause treaties that contain some contractual clauses and some lawmaking clauses. For this reason some authorities refuse to distinguish between the two types and regard all treaties as sources of international law.

Treaties are the main tools of cooperation in international relations. The United States currently has in effect approximately 3,800 bilateral treaties with 138 different nations ranging alphabetically from Afghanistan to Zambia, and with eighteen international organizations ranging alphabetically from the Agency for the Safety of Air Navigation in Africa and Madagascar to the United Nations. It is also signatory to more than 375 multilateral treaties on more than eighty-five different subjects. In 1972 alone the United States entered into 315 new treaty arrangements.

Many treaties are short-term and automatically expire on specified dates unless extended by subsequent agreement. Others are for specific transactions and are no longer operative when such transactions have been completed. In this area was the already mentioned grain agreement with the Soviet Union of July 8, 1972.

The first two treaties ever negotiated by the United States were with France and were signed during the Revolutionary War, before the United States had actually gained independence but had been recognized as an independent nation by France. The treaties were signed on February 6, 1778, and were ratified by Congress on May 4, 1778. One was a treaty of amity and commerce, the other a treaty of alliance, which was to go into effect only if Great Britain declared war on France. Neither treaty remains in effect today, although neither was ever formally terminated. The reasons for their demise, which do not reflect very favorably on the United States, are given in Chapter V.

If circumstances do not change, a treaty with no termination date remains in effect indefinitely unless terminated by mutual agreement or disavowed by one of the contracting parties. It is also possible for a portion of a treaty to remain in force when other parts of it have become obsolete because of changed circumstances. Thus three articles of the Jay Treaty of 1794 (between the United States and Great Britain) that pertain to Canada still remain in force. The other articles, which involved such matters as the surrender of certain frontier posts held by the British, claims for confiscated debts, and reciprocal claims for the illegal seizure of American ships by the British and the seizure of British ships by French ships armed in American ports, have long since become obsolete.

The United States has more treaties with Canada— more than 300—than with any other nation. In contrast we have fewer than 65 treaties in force with the only other bordering nation, Mexico. The nation with which we have the second largest number of treaties—about 180—is the United Kingdom. To cite a few more nations at random, we have about 90 treaties each with France and Japan, some 75 with Italy, and a little more than 40 with the Soviet Union. With other nations we have only a few treaties in effect, and with a few less-developed nations we have only one treaty each. With Algeria, for instance, we have only a single agricultural commodity agreement, with Bahrain only a defense treaty, with Bangladesh only a treaty granting U.S. economic and technical aid, with Brunei only a treaty of peace, commerce, and friendship.

The more than four thousand bilateral and multilateral treaties to which the United States is a signatory range over a wide variety of subjects. Just to give some idea of that range, here are the subjects of the twenty treaties we have in force with Afghanistan:

Seven are agreements concerning the sale or purchase of agricultural commodities. Four concern economic and technical aid to be furnished by the United States to Afghanistan. The other nine concern the diverse subjects of cultural relations, defense, educational exchange programs, diplomatic and consular relations, guarantees of freedom of information, investment guarantees to

American industries investing in Afghanistan, the establishment of a Peace Corps in that nation, the exchange of official publications, and duty-free entry into Afghanistan of relief supplies for the natives.

When a treaty enters into force, it becomes not only international law but a part of the municipal law of the signatory nations. For example, the United States being a party to the Geneva Conventions requires its citizens to observe them. The mistreatment of a prisoner of war by a United States soldier will be deemed a breach of international law by the United States on an international level, but it is also a crime by the soldier under the municipal law of the United States.

In nations such as the United States, where legislative ratification of treaties is required, such ratification automatically makes a treaty the law of the land because it is a legislative act. But in nations such as England, where ratification is not required, special legislation is sometimes required either to repeal municipal law in conflict with treaty provisions or to add new law in order to conform to such provisions. In practice the usual custom in such circumstances is simply to withhold signature to the treaty until the necessary legislation can be passed to bring the law of the land into conformity with the treaty.

Depending on the differing municipal law of nations, treaties become binding on signatories by three different means: upon signature, upon ratification, or by accession.

In nations where the head of state has the sole treaty-making power or is empowered to delegate such authority to ministers, a treaty goes into effect as soon as it is signed (or on a specific date after signing, if that is a treaty provision). This is the situation in the United Kingdom, where municipal law provides that the power to make treaties belongs to the Queen, acting on the advice of her ministers.

In other nations legislative ratification is required before treaties become law. The United States Constitution requires ratification by a two-thirds majority of the Senate. United States treaties are customarily signed by some diplomat designated by the President or the Secretary of State, but do not enter into force until ratified.

Accession is the acceptance of the terms of a treaty by a nation that was not a party to the drawing up of the treaty. This is possible only if the treaty provides for this procedure, and will be discussed in more detail a few paragraphs farther on.

Bilateral treaties in most cases create only what is called *particular law,* as opposed to *general law,* in that they create international law only between the two signatories, and obviously make no universal law applicable to all nations. However, if a sufficient number of bilateral treaties of a similar nature are concluded, they may attain the force of general law. For instance, since every nation in the world has at least some treaties with other nations providing for the extradition of criminals, these separate bilateral treaties, lumped together, have come to have the collective force of general international law.

Obviously multilateral treaties are more effective in creating general law, and these have come into steadily increasing use since the end of World War I. Some of these, such as the agreements under the North Atlantic Treaty Organization (NATO) or the Organization of American States (OAS) are regional in nature. Others formulated under the sponsorship of the United Nations have worldwide effect.

These latter agreements, usually called conventions, generally have two things in common. One is that they attempt to codify the law in the area with which the convention is concerned, with the goal of gaining universal acceptance of rules and principles on that subject. The other is that they include a clause inviting nations that have not participated in the framing of the convention to become party to it by accession.

No better illustration can be given as to how such conventions come into effect than to give the background of the one that is concerned with treaty-making itself. This is called the Vienna Convention on the Law of Treaties.

Over the centuries treaties to some extent have come to follow similar form and to employ similar terminology, no matter in what part of the world they were drawn up or in what language. There have never been strict rules about this, however, or even closely observed custom. It has never even been a requirement of international law that they be written, and even today there are some oral treaties in effect that are regarded as having the same legal force as written agreements.

Following World War II there was a general feeling among both long-established nations and emerging new nations that an international code was needed to standardize the drawing up of treaties. In 1949 the International Law Commission began to study the matter and to draft a proposed treaty, a project that consumed nearly eighteen years.

In 1966 the United Nations General Assembly, on the basis of the International Law Commission's report, adopted a resolution convening a United Nations Conference on the Law of Treaties, to begin in 1968 and to be held at Vienna. One hundred and ten nations were represented at the conference, which met for two separate two-month sessions, the first in the spring of 1968, the second a year later.

On May 23, 1969, the conference adopted the Vienna Convention on the Law of Treaties. It was signed for the United States on April 24, 1970, and was transmitted to the Senate for ratification by President Richard Nixon on November 22, 1971. As of the fall of 1973 it had still not been ratified, but almost certainly will be.

The treaty provides that it shall enter into force thirty days after the deposit of its signing, ratification, or accession by the thirty-fifth nation accepting it. As has become the custom for all such conventions sponsored by the United Nations, that organization is named as the depository.

As of this writing thirty-five acceptances have not yet been deposited, but nevertheless the convention already has the force of law, because most nations are following the procedures laid down in the treaty in anticipation that it will be in force before long. It is just that the wheels of diplomacy, like the wheels of justice, sometimes grind exceedingly slow. Many more than thirty-five nations have *signed* the treaty, but there have not yet been sufficient ratifications and accessions to enter it into force.

The Vienna Convention is too long to report even in comprehensive résumé, so merely a couple of its highlights will be touched upon. It does not affect treaties already in force, whose legal statuses remain unchanged, but stipulates that all future treaties will be in *written* form and in the format laid down by the convention. It further sets certain rules designed to insure strict observance of treaties by the signatories. In example, Article 18 provides:

> A state is obliged to refrain from acts which would defeat the object and purpose of a treaty when:
>
> (a) It has signed the treaty or has exchanged instruments constituting the treaty subject to ratification, acceptance or approval, until it has made its intention clear not to become a party to the treaty; or
>
> (b) It has expressed its consent to be bound by the treaty pending the entry into force of the treaty and provided that such entry into force is not unduly delayed.

Although partially contested by the communist nations, it is a generally held principle of international law that a change in regime, or even a complete change of government through revolution or conquest, does not relieve a nation of treaty obligations made prior to the change. Under this principle treaties executed by the Batista regime in Cuba remained binding on the communist government of Fidel Castro after the revolution there. Even former colonies that have gained independence are held by most nations, particularly among the Western nations, to continue to be bound by treaties concerning their own territories that were executed by their mother countries before they gained independence. The Republic of the Philippines, for instance, is still bound by certain treaties made by the United States before it became independent on July 4, 1946, but only when such treaties apply directly to its geographical territory. A mutual defense pact signed by the United States prior to July 4, 1946, could not commit the Republic of the Philippines to go to war when the United States did, even though its territory was possessed by the United States at that time. But various extradition treaties executed by the United States that specifically agreed to extradition procedures for the Philippine Islands still remain in effect for the Republic of the Philippines.

In a world whose political makeup has been changing as rapidly as ours since World War II, quite obviously this principle is important to the continuity of international relations.

Custom

In the field of international law *customary law* is very similar to common law in the area of municipal law. Common law, it will be recalled, was defined as "custom so widespread and so generally accepted that it has the force of law." Customary law may be defined as custom accepted among nations, either worldwide or by specific groups of nations, which through precedent and general acceptance has the force of international law. The qualifying phrase "either worldwide or by specific groups of nations" is important here, for it is possible for specific rules of customary law to be recognized by some nations and be rejected by others.

It is also possible for the custom of a single nations to establish customary law applicable to that particular nation only. In making claims before either an international or a municipal tribunal, it is a valid argument for the claimant to show what the defendant nation's customary practice has been under similar circumstances, and it is equally valid for the defendant nation to advance its customary practice in defense of its actions. Examples of judicial decisions based on both general customary law and particular customary law follow.

In 1898, at the beginning of the Spanish-American War, two fishing smacks working out of Havana, flying the Spanish flag, were captured by U.S. warships blockading the Cuban coast when they attempted to return to Havana. The fishing vessels were unarmed, and the crews were unaware that Spain and the United States had gone to war. The smacks were taken to Key West, condemned as prizes of war by a district court of the United States, and were sold.

The owners appealed to the U.S. Supreme Court.

In the 1900 Supreme Court decision of *The Paquete Habana and the Lola v. the United States* Justice Horace Gray delivered the majority opinion, which said in part: "By ancient usage among civilized nations, beginning centuries ago, and gradually ripening into a rule of international law, coast fishing vessels, pursuing their vocations of catching and bringing in fresh fish, have been recognized as exempt, with their cargoes and crews, from capture as prizes of war."

Justice Gray noted that this doctrine had been "earnestly contested at the bar," and cited examples of such contestings, but held that the weight of precedent made it a general rule of international law. The decree of the district court was reversed, the proceeds of the sale of the vessels and their cargoes were ordered paid to the claimants, and they were further allowed damages and costs.

The Anglo-Norwegian Fisheries Case, instituted by the British Government before the International Court of Justice in 1949 and decided in 1951, is an example of the application of particular customary law.

The distance out into the ocean from shore claimed by nations as their territorial waters and recognized as such by other nations varies from nation to nation. Norway happens to claim four miles.

Ever since 1911 Norway had periodically been seizing British fishing vessels operating off its coast, allegedly for violating the prohibition against fishing within Norway's territorial waters. Britain protested that many of the seizures occurred beyond the four-mile limit and therefore took place on the high seas. The point of contention centered around Norway's method of computing the outer boundary of its territorial waters. Because of the peculiar irregularity of its coastline, the Norwegian practice was to draw the outer boundary four miles from an imaginary base line that followed the general direction of the coast, but ignored indentations. Britain objected that because Norway had never claimed more than a four-mile limit, the principle of customary practice fixed the limits of its territorial waters at that distance from shore, but its method of computing included some waters several miles farther out than that.

The Court upheld Norway's position, but to avoid establishing a precedent that might encourage other nations to expand their territorial waters by adopting Norway's system of computation, thus bringing on a spate of similar disputes, its opinion was carefully worded to make clear that circumstances were unique in this instance and that the straight base-line method was not universally applicable. Norway's practice had consistently been to compute the outer boundary of its territorial waters in this manner, and therefore it was particular customary law. A nation that had never used this method of computation could not now begin to use it simply to gain more territorial water. The law on this has since changed, and many nations now use the straight baseline method of computation.

American jurist Samuel Chase, in an eighteenth-century judicial opinion, said, "Cusom is only obligatory on those nations who have adopted it." Lord Alverstone, Chief Justice of the King's Bench Division in England, in a 1905 judicial opinion said that any customary rule of international law that "has been so widely and generally accepted that it can hardly be supposed that any civilized state would repudiate it, is binding on England." These opposing statements not only illustrate the divergence of opinion among authorities but are interesting in relation to their times. During the lifetime of Samuel Chase, the bulk of international law consisted of customary law. In Lord Alverstone's day treaties had become a more important source of international law than custom, and it was the era of power politics and the doctrine of absolute sovereignty. It is therefore rather intriguing that a noted jurist of that period would find international custom to which his nation had not necessarily agreed "binding" on it.

The same difference of opinion lingers on today. The practices of international courtesy, such as honoring visiting heads of state with twenty-one-gun salutes, are universally accepted as customary law, but are customary law in its simplest and least controversial form, because such rules are unlikely to impinge on national self-interest. No point could be gained by a nation stubbornly insisting on a twenty- or twenty-two-gun salute for heads of state. It is only when you get into practices that can affect national interests that you run into differences of opinion.

The thorniest problem is how many instances of a particular practice must occur before it may be deemed a rule of customary law. In both the cases of customary law cited above, the evidence is clear that both the general practice and the particular practice concerned go back many years. But at what point does a nation's action under specific circumstances become a customary rule? Examining legal precedents isn't very helpful in deciding.

In 1948 Victor Raúl Haya de la Torre, leader of a Peruvian political party called America's Popular Revolutionary Alliance, took refuge in the Colombian embassy in Lima to escape arrest for his part in a milirary rebellion. As it had long been a rule of customary law that nations need not extradite persons accused only of political crimes, Colombia granted asylum and requested Peru to give Haya de la Torre safe conduct out of the country. Peru disputed the right of Colombia to decide solely upon its own judgment that the man was a political refugee instead of a common criminal, then expect Peru to accept its judgment. The case was referred to the International Court of Justice. (ICJ)

Only one part of the judicial opinion rendered in this case is important to the present discussion, and because it was an involved case with many ramifications, we will not go into the rest of the opinion. However, to satisfy reader curiosity as to the eventual fate of Haya de la Torre, events will be briefly summarized. After an initial decision by the International Court of Justice that left the matter somewhat up in the air, Colombia requested and got a second decision, which failed to clarify matters very much. Eventually Colombia and Peru negotiated an agreement between themselves under which Haya de la Torre was allowed to leave the country secretly. In 1962 he returned to Peru and unsuccessfully ran for President.

The one part of the 1950 opinion in the Asylum Case of interest to us here is the statement that a customary rule must be based on "a constant and uniform usage."

On the other hand, in the 1953 case of the *Anglo-Iranian Oil Company v. Societá Unione Petrolifera Orientale,* a dispute between an English and an Italian company over ownership of some oil, the Civil Tribunal of Venice found for the Italian firm on the basis of a rule of customary law based on a single resolution of the U.N. General Assembly concerning the nationalization of foreign-owned industries.

To go one step further, another General Assembly resolution requires nations launching space satellites to pay for any damages to other nations caused by such launchings. No claims have yet been made under this resolution, but some authorities predict that if and when they are made, they will be made on the basis that the General Assembly resolution created customary law. If that premise gains general acceptance, there will be the odd legal concept that no precedent at all is required in at least some circumstances in order to create customary law, but it may exist in advance of any actual occurrence by virtue of prior general acceptance of a hypothetical principle.

Despite the inability of nations and authorities to agree on just what constitutes customary law, it is an important area of international law because it is frequently cited by both claimant and defendant nations in disputes, and frequently is the basis on which both international and municipal courts render judicial opinions.

The areas of disagreement are gradually disappearing anyway, because of a growing tendency to codify customary law in international conventions. The Vienna

Convention on the Law of Treaties is an example of this trend, in that by incorporating the customary law concerning treaties, it virtually wiped out the customary law in that area by converting it to codified law. As more and more conventions of this nature come into effect, it can be expected that customary law will become less and less important for the simple reason that there will be little of it that has not been formalized into codified rules by treaties.

GENERAL PRINCIPLES OF LAW

The courts of the United states and of other common-law nations commonly apply general principles of law (i.e, legal precedents) in handing down decisions. However, as has been pointed out, precedents are not binding on the courts of civil-law nations. In phrasing the Statute of the International Court of Justice its framers had to take into consideration that the Court would be serving nations with different types of legal systems, and therefore felt that statutory authorization was needed to make available to the justices of the ICJ this resource to which the judges in common-law nations regarded themselves as automatically entitled without requiring special statutory permission.

The motive of the statesmen who drafted the Statute was to provide possible solution in cases where treaties and customary law gave insufficient guidance, and it is quite clear that they meant the Court to review previous legal decisions and use them as guidelines in such instances. However, as in all areas of international law, there is considerable disagreement as to the exact meaning of the phrase "the general principles of law recognized by civilized nations." Some say it means general principles of international law, some that it refers to the general principles of the municipal law of all nations, others that it means the general principles of both.

Seemingly the justices of the ICJ themselves are in the third category, since they have applied both municipal-law and international-law precedents in rendering opinions. They have the weight of customary law on their side in this, as the Permanent Court of International Justice (PCIJ), the ancestor under the League of Nations of the present Court, also applied both types of law. For that matter international tribunals were applying both types of law long before the PCIJ was created in 1920.

Unfortunately in cases before the International Court of Justice or other international tribunals involving the Soviet Union, that nation insists that the term "general principles of law" means only the most basic principles of law stemming from treaty and custom, and does not include legal precedents derived from previous judicial opinions. The fact that the ICJ Statute lists general principles of law as a source separate from treaties and customs, and therefore could not logically have been meant to include only principles stemming from those two sources, does not shake Russia's insistence on its own point of view. No nation outside of the communist world accepts the Russian view, but nevertheless, since arbitration by the ICJ requires mutual consent, noncommunist nations in disputes with the Soviet Union sometimes have to accept the restriction that the Court will not consider legal precedents in order to get their disputes before the Court at all.

JUDICIAL DECISIONS AND THE TEACHINGS OF PUBLICISTS

At first glance it might seem puzzling that Russia refuses to accept legal precedents as a source of law under the previous clause, yet has no objection to "judicial decisions . . . as subsidiary means for the determination of rules of law." The answer is that under this clause judicial decisions are not considered from the point of view of establishing legal precedents, but merely as sources of information for the justices.

Linking such decisions with "the teachings of the

most highly qualified publicists of the various nations" makes this clear. "Publicists" is merely international-lawyer talk for professors of international law and other scholarly writers on the subject. Obviously the opinions of these writers cannot make law, but can only furnish guidance. (In the past writers such as Grotius exercised such vast influence that in a sense they made law, but those days are long past. No modern writer could hope to be so influential.) Under this clause judicial decisions are regarded as bearing no more weight than writers' opinions. That is, they are merely resources for guidance, no more binding upon the ICJ than textbooks on international law. The fact that both sources are to be used only as "subsidiary means for the determination of rules of law" makes this even more evident.

Clause (d) begins, "Subject to the provisions of Article 59." Article 59 of the Statute of the ICJ states in part, "The decision of the Court has no binding force except between the parties and in respect of that particular case." In other words, while clause (c), at least in the view of nations of the Western world, permits the justices to consider legal precedents of other courts, the decisions of the ICJ itself do not constitute precedents. This can only be explained as the influence of those representatives among the framers of the statute from civil-law nations, whose legal systems, it will be recalled, do not hold precedents binding. It is one of the anomalies that can be expected in a legal system developed by representatives of so many different nations with differing systems of law.

OTHER SOURCES

As has been mentioned, some authorities object to the limitations set down by Article 38(1) as to sources of international law. While there is no general agreement that the following are valid sources of international law, they are included as sources by many writers.

As was indicated in the section on customary law,

resolutions by the General Assembly of the United Nations may create international law. The very fact that a resolution passed indicates acceptance of the principle laid down by the member nations. Objectors to including such resolutions as sources of law point out that the United Nations has no legislative power, and therefore its resolutions do not have the force of law. Admittedly they are not laws in the same sense that acts by the legislatures of nations are laws, but if they are generally accepted by the member nations as guides to international conduct, it is mere quibbling to deny them the status of international law.

Practices of international organizations may also create customary law. For example, the United Nations Secretariat is generally named as the depository of signatures, ratifications, and accessions to conventions. More and more it is becoming the practice to include a clause in all treaties, including bilateral ones, naming the Secretariat as the depository, a practice that has altered the customary law concerning treaties.

Article 38(2) of the Statute of the ICJ provides that the list of sources of international law in Article 38(1) "shall not prejudice the power of the Court to decide a case *ex aequo et bono* [according to what is just and good] if the parties agree thereto." This means that the court decision may be based on the principle of equity alone, but only if application of the principle is specifically authorized by the contesting parties.

There is a growing tendency among international arbitrators and jurists to feel that when no rule based on treaty or custom is available to settle a dispute, decision should be based simply on the principle of justice. However, so far this has been applied only in instances where the principle of equity does not conflict with treaty provisions or customary law. The principle of *ex aequo et bono* implies that justice should be the *sole* consideration, overriding all other factors. And Article 38(2) has never been put into effect because disputing parties have never authorized the ICJ to apply it.

For this reason some authorities deny that equity is a

source of international law. Nevertheless, a growing number of authorities believe that nations have definite moral responsibilities in their dealings with other nations. So however nebulous its impact may be, equity does seem to be at least a minor source of international law.

Chapter III

THE UNITED NATIONS

The most important agency of international cooperation is the United Nations. Its charter was drafted at San Francisco in 1945 by representatives of fifty-one nations, all on the Allied side in World War II. It provided that membership was open to all other peace-loving nations that accept the obligations contained in the Charter and, in the judgment of the United Nations, are able and willing to carry out these obligations. Approval by both the General Assembly and the Security Council is necessary for new members to be admitted.

Currently there are 135 members of the United Nations. Almost all the independent nations of the world except the two divided nations of Korea and Vietnam, a few very small nations, and Switzerland now belong. The two divided nations and the small ones have been excluded by vote of the members, but Switzerland has never applied. Its reason is that it feels membership would be incompatible with its traditional policy of neutrality and would decrease its ability to act as a disinterested go-between in times of war.

The purposes of the United Nations are given in Article 1 of its charter:

1. To maintain international peace and security, and to that end: to take effective collective measures for the prevention and removal of threats to the peace and for the suppression of acts of aggression or other breaches of the peace, and to bring about by peaceful means, and in conformity with the principles of justice and international law, adjustment or settlement of international disputes or

situations which might lead to a breach of the peace.

2. To develop friendly relations among nations based on respect for the principle of equal rights and self-determination of peoples, and to take other appropriate measures to strengthen universal peace.

3. To achieve international cooperation in solving international problems of an economic, social, cultural or humanitarian character, and in promoting and encouraging respect for human rights and for the fundamental freedoms of all without distinction as to race, sex, language or religion; and

4. To be a center for harmonizing the actions of nations in the attainment of these common ends.

There are six principal organs of the United Nations, plus a large number of subsidiary organs under the principal ones.

THE SECURITY COUNCIL

The Security Council consists of fifteen member nations. Five are permanent members; the other ten are elected for two-year terms by the General Assembly. There is informal understanding that five of the nonpermanent seats go to Afro-Asian nations, two to Latin America, one to some East European nation, and two to West European nations or nations in friendly accord with West European nations (meaning predominantly white nations such as Australia and Canada).

Originally the five permanent members were France, the United Kingdom, the Soviet Union, the United States, and Nationalist China. But on October 25, 1971, the General Assembly adopted a draft resolution sponsored by twenty-three nations by a vote of 76 to 35, with 17 abstentions (there were then only 128 member nations), recognizing representatives of the People's Republic of China as the only lawful representatives of China, and expelled the representatives of Nationalist

China. Communist China therefore now holds the permanent seat in the Security Council originally held by Nationalist China.

This act is widely spoken of as the "admission" of the People's Republic of China to the United Nations. But that is not quite correct. The People's Republic was not admitted as a new member, but was merely recognized as the only legal representative of the Chinese people to the United Nations. The resolution states that it is *restoring* its rights to the People's Republic of China and expelling "forthwith the representatives of Chiang Kai-shek from the place which they unlawfully occupy at the United Nations and in all the organizations related to it."

The main function of the Security Council is to maintain world peace. To this end it makes recommendations for the peaceful settlement of disputes and is empowered to take certain enforcement actions to deal with either threats to peace or actual breaches of it. Enforcement actions include economic sanctions and military "police actions." An example of the former was the 1966 order to member states to suspend trade in some commodities with Southern Rhodesia. An example of the latter was the 1950 resolution recommending that member states "furnish such assistance to the Republic of Korea as may be necessary to repel the armed attack [by North Korea] and to restore international peace."

One of the criticisms of the old League of Nations was that "it had no teeth in it"—that its enforcement procedures simply did not work. Its biggest weakness was that each member nation was allowed to be its own judge of whether or not a particular act constituted a threat to peace or breach of peace

Article 39 of the U.N. Charter provides: "The Security Council shall determine the existence of any threat to peace, breach of the peace, or act of aggression and shall make recommendations, or decide what measures shall be taken . . . to maintain or restore international peace and security." Article 25 provides: "The members of the United Nations agree to accept and carry out the decisions of the Security Council in accordance with the present Charter." In other words the Security Council is the sole judge of what is a threat to peace, a breach of the peace, or an act of aggression, and it has the power to make its decisions legally binding on the member nations.

This would seem to give it considerably more clout as a peace-keeping agency than the League of Nations ever possessed, but checking that power is the veto power given the five permanent members. Article 27 of the U.N. Charter provides that on purely procedural matters any nine votes carry a decision. But on other matters, although only nine votes are still required, all five of the permanent members must be included among the nine, unless one or more abstain from voting.

In short, each permanent member has absolute veto power on nonprocedural matters.

The Western press has criticized Russia for using its veto power much more often than the other permanent members have. But the statistics on this are misleading because, until October 25, 1971, the other four permanent members have generally been in accord against Russia on political issues, and when one or more of them wanted to defeat an issue, usually it was possible to muster enough support among nonpermanent members to vote it down, so that exercise of the veto was not required. In instances where they were unable to gain sufficient support, the other four were usually as quick to use the veto as Russia. For instance, in 1956 France and the United Kingdom vetoed a resolution condemning the seizure of the Suez Canal.

What effect the replacement of Nationalist China by the People's Republic of China as a permanent member will have on the use of the veto power is a matter of conjecture. At the moment China seems to be more in the camp of the Western powers than with Russia, with whom she is having serious disagreements. But ideologically China is so far apart from the United Kingdom, France, and the United States that it is difficult to visualize her consistently siding with those powers against her fellow communist nation.

Suggestions that the veto be abolished in order to

make the United Nations work better are probably un-realistic. Although nations today do not play as raw power politics as they did prior to World War I, power politics is by no means merely a matter of historical curiosity, and the veto provision is a realistic acceptance that it still exists. It is far more likely that instead of strengthening the United Nations, abolition of the veto would destroy it, because it is unlikely that any of the five permanent members—all nuclear powers—would docilely submit to any enforcement procedures voted against them.

THE GENERAL ASSEMBLY

The General Assembly consists of representatives of all the member nations, each with equal vote. The United Nations Charter gives the General Assembly a much wider range of interests than the Security Council, but not as much power. It is authorized to "discuss" a wide variety of subjects including "any questions relating to the maintenance of international peace and security brought before it . . . and . . . may make recommendations with regard to any such question to the state or states concerned or to the Security Council or both."

Article 13(1) of the U.N. Charter states:

The General Assembly shall initiate studies and make recommendations for the purpose of:
(a) Promoting international cooperation in the political field and encouraging the progressive development of international law and its codification;
(b) Promoting international cooperation in the economic, social, cultural, educational and health fields and assisting in the realization of human rights and basic freedoms for all without distinction as to race, sex, language or religion.

Article 14 provides: ". . . the General Assembly may recommend measures for the peaceful adjustment of any situation, regardless of origin, which it deems likely to impair the general welfare or friendly relations among nations. . . ."

A two-thirds vote of the General Assembly is required for decisions on specified subjects, which include: international peace and security, the election of nonpermanent members of the Security Council and of members of the Economic and Social Council and of the Trusteeship Council, the admission of new members to the United Nations, the suspension of rights and privileges of membership, the expulsion of members, and budgetary matters. Decisions on other matters, including the addition of other subjects that will require a two-thirds majority, are by a simple majority vote of the members present.

Of matters concerned solely with the operation of the United Nations, such as fixing the annual budget, the General Assembly may make decisions that are binding on the member nations. But in political matters, such as disputes between nations, it can only make recommendations and has no power to enforce such recommendations. The sole power to enforce U.N. decisions lies with the Security Council. For this reason there is no veto power in the General Assembly. Since its recommendations are not binding, veto isn't needed.

Even though its recommendations are not binding, they may exert great influence. A resolution condemning the action of a nation as illegal under international law may cause the condemned nation to cease its illegal action. Or even the mere threat of such condemnation may cause a nation to refrain from an illegal action. Because no nation cares to be the subject of worldwide public outrage, the mere capacity of the General Assembly to pass such resolutions acts as a deterrent to violations of international law.

The Economic and Social Council

The Economic and Social Council is the organ through which the General Assembly discharges its charter obligation to promote international cooperation in "the economic, social, cultural, educational and health fields and . . . in the realization of human rights and basic freedoms. . . ." The members of the Council are elected by the General Assembly, and the Council is directly responsible to that body.

Originally the Economic and Social Council consisted of eighteen members. In 1966 it was increased to twenty-seven, and a recent amendment to Article 61 of the U.N. Charter doubles its present membership to fifty-four. This amendment required ratification by two-thirds of the member nations, including all five of the permanent members of the Security Council. It entered into force September 24, 1973, when the ninety-third ratification was deposited by the United States.

Members serve for three-year terms, one third of them being elected by the General Assembly each year.

The Council is empowered by the U.N. Charter to make studies and reports concerning international economic, social, cultural, educational, and health fields, to make recommendations promoting human rights and fundamental freedoms, and to draft conventions relating to these matters for submission to the General Assembly. It may also call international conferences on matters within its competence. Like the General Assembly, it has only advisory power and cannot make decisions binding on the member nations.

In carrying out its functions the Economic and Social Council acts as coordinator of a large number of specialized international agencies. Some of these agencies were formed by the General Assembly, and one was spawned by the Economic and Social Council itself, but most of them were originally created separately from the United Nations (some even predate the U.N.) and have voluntarily placed themselves under the control of the Economic and Social Council by written agreement. These agreements vary in terms, but in general provide that the agencies will send regular reports of their activities to the Economic and Social Council and will consider recommendations concerning their actions made by both the Economic and Social Council and the General Assembly. Currently these specialized agencies include the following:

The Food and Agricultural Organization (FAO), formed in 1943, has the function of collecting and distributing information on nutrition, food, and agriculture and of promoting conservation policies to preserve the world's natural resources.

The Inter-Governmental Maritime Consultive Organization (IMCO) was formed in 1958 to provide machinery for cooperation among nations in matters concerning shipping, maritime safety, and navigational efficiency and to promote the removal of unfair and discriminatory practices in international trade.

The International Bank for Reconstruction and Development (IBRD), better known as the World Bank, was created in 1945 to promote the international flow of capital for productive purposes, to assist in financing the reconstruction of areas devastated by war, and to further the economic development of the member nations.

The International Civil Aviation Organization (ICAO) was established in 1947 to coordinate and provide means for setting international standards for air navigational equipment, both ground and air.

The International Labor Organization (ILO), originally formed under the League of Nations in 1919, attempts to improve worldwide labor conditions by promoting international standards for such matters as hours of labor, the protection of women and children in industry, industrial safety measures, and workmen's compensation.

The International Monetary Fund (IMF) was created in 1945 to promote international monetary cooperation, to establish stable exchange rates among the currencies of the world, and to promote international trade and a high level of employment throughout the world.

The International Telecommunications Satellite Organization (INTELSAT) was created by multilateral treaty at Washington, D.C., in 1971 but was not ratified by the United States and did not go into effect until February 12, 1973. The organization supervises the use of communications satellites in orbit around the earth that are used for the relay of radio and television signals.

The International Telecommunications Union (ITU) was founded in 1865 and became a specialized agency of the United Nations in 1947. It works to assure the free flow of radio communications by registering all radio frequencies in order to eliminate unnecessary interference and arranges cooperation between the various nations in the assignment of frequencies.

The United Nations Children's Fund (UNICEF) was established by the U.N. General Assembly in 1946, under its former name of the United Nations International Children's Emergency Fund, as a temporary agency to provide relief for mothers and children in areas devastated during World War II. In 1953 it was made a permanent agency for the relief of children and mothers in areas devastated during any war, and its name was changed to the present one. Because by then it was so well known by its initials, UNICEF, that acronym was retained.

The United Nations Educational Scientific and Cultural Organization (UNESCO) was established in 1945 to promote collaboration among nations in raising educational levels, in the exchange of scientific information, and in cultural exchange.

The Universal Postal Union (UPU), founded in 1874, became a specialized agency of the United Nations in 1947. Its purpose is to achieve greater uniformity in postal relations between nations and to plan new means to expedite mail delivery.

The World Health Organization (WHO) was established in 1948 under the auspices of the Economic and Social Council for the purpose of improving world health. It combats widespread diseases such as malaria and promotes the improvement of nutrition, housing, mental health, and maternal and child walfare.

The World Meterological Organization (WMO) was established by the General Assembly in 1950 to set international procedures, standards, and practices for weather observation stations throughout the world.

THE INTERNATIONAL COURT OF JUSTICE (ICJ)

The International Court of Justice was established by Articles 92 through 96 of the Charter of the United Nations, but its composition and functions are outlined in the Statute of the International Court of Justice, which is annexed to and forms and integral part of the Charter. The Statute is based on the statute of the old Permanent Court of International Justice under the League of Nations, and is very similar.

All members of the United Nations are automatically parties to the Statute. It is also possible for a nonmember nation to become party to it upon recommendation by the Security Council and approval by the General Assembly. Under certain circumstances nonmember nations who are not even party to the Statute may appear before the Court. These last two circumstances are becoming increasingly rare, though, because there are not many nations left in the world that are not now members of the United Nations.

The Court consists of fifteen judges, no two of whom may be citizens of the same nation. They are elected by secret ballot in concurrent session of the Security Council and the General Assembly. The vote of both organs must be by majority of the total membership, not merely a majority of those present.

In addition to the fifteen elected judges, when a nation that does not have a judge on the court appears as a litigant, it may appoint one *ad hoc* (for this case only) from its own nation.

Terms for the elected judges are nine years, but in order to provide for some continuity in the composition of the Court, at the first election, in 1946, five members were elected for three years, five for six years, and five for nine years. Ever since, five members have been elected every three years for the full term.

There is informal agreement that all permanent members of the Security Council always have a judge on the Court, a makeup that has varied only once in the

Court's history. That variation, however, has managed to keep the newest permanent member of the Security Council from having a seat.

In 1966 Nationalist China did not nominate anyone, and a candidate from the Republic of the Philippines was elected instead. If Nationalist China had held a seat at the time the General Assembly expelled it from the United Nations, that seat would have gone to the People's Republic of China, because the resolution expelled Nationalist China not only from the United Nations but "from all organizations related to it," and replaced all Nationalist Chinese representatives with representatives from the People's Republic of China. The Philippine judge's term expires in 1976, however, and China will undoubtedly fill that seat.

The last election was held October 30, 1972, for five judges whose terms began February 6, 1973, and run until 1982. These five are from Argentina, France, India, Senegal, and the United Kingdom. The five whose terms expire in 1979 are from Dahomey, Spain, Uruguay, the Soviet Union, and the United States. The U.S. judge is Hardy C. Dillard. The five whose terms expire in 1976 are from Lebanon, Nigeria, Poland, the Republic of the Philippines, and Sweden.

The Court does not sit at the site of the United Nations in New York City, but at The Hague, in the Netherlands.

Under the U.N. Charter and the Statute of the ICJ, only nations may bring disputes before the Court. However, the Security Council and the General Assembly may request advisory opinions on points of law, and other organs of the United Nations and its specialized agencies may also request such opinions, if authorized to do so by the General Assembly.

Nations appear before the Court only by their own consent, but once having accepted the jurisdiction of the Court, they are bound by its decision. Article 94 states, "Each member of the United Nations undertakes to comply with the decision of the International Court of Justice in any case to which it is a party," then further provides that the injured nation may request the Security Council to enforce judgment if the defendant nation fails to perform its obligation under the Court's decision.

Actually no nation has ever had to ask the Security Council to take enforcement action to require performance of a court decision, because in the only case of refusal there was no point in it. Great Britain did not press her judgment against Albania in the Corfu Channel Case, described a little further on, because she knew the Soviet Union would veto any attempt to apply sanctions against Albania, and there was no point in stirring up international resentments over a lost cause.

This has been the single case of a nation refusing to abide by a decision of the International Court of Justice, because defendant nations do not consent to appear before the Court as a general rule unless they are willing to abide by its decisions. From the standpoint of world opinion, they would be much wiser to refuse its jurisdiction in the first place then to accept it and then reject its decisions.

Another factor that is probably at least partly responsible for this high rate of compliance is simply pragmatic recognition by the Court of the limitation of its enforcement power. Whereas a municipal court may base its decisions solely upon the evidence and the principles of justice, international tribunals must also take into consideration the acceptability of their decisions to all parties concerned. There is therefore a tendency to compromise between absolute justice and what the defendant will accept. On the pragmatic principle that half a loaf is better than none, plaintiff nations tend to accept such compromise decisions also. The plaintiff nation usually realizes that a favorable decision, even if not fully satisfactory, is the best it could reasonably expect, because if it were any more favorable, the defendant nation might refuse to comply. From a practical point of view the net effect of that on the plaintiff would be the same as having lost the case.

There are several ways in which nations may give their consent to appear before the Court. Quite often consent is given in advance of any dispute by inclusion of a clause in treaties stipulating that disputes arising as to the meaning or performance of the treaties will be referred to the Court for interpretation, although it is more common for such clauses to call for referral to an arbitral commission. Where there is no such treaty clause, a dispute may be referred to the Court by mutual agreement. But it is also possible for a defendant nation to accept the jurisdiction of the Court after a proceeding has been entered against it, even though the proceeding was started unilaterally by the claimant nation without the consent of the defendant nation. The Corfu Channel Case is an example.

On October 22, 1946, two British destroyers were damaged by permanently anchored mines in the channel between the island of Corfu and Albania, in Albanian territorial waters. Great Britain charged that Albania knew the minefield was there, and its failure to warn other nations of its existence was a violation of the Eighth Hague Convention of 1907. Great Britain demanded payment of compensation in the amount of £875,000 for damages and loss of life.

Albania countered that the presence of British warships in its territorial waters without prior authorization was a breach of international law, and therefore Britain's claim was invalid.

On May 22, 1947, Great Britain instituted proceedings against the People's Republic of Albania before the International Court of Justice. Albania filed an objection.

On December 9, 1947, the Court rejected the objection filed by Albania and simultaneously held that the filing of the objection constituted acceptance of the jurisdiction of the Court. Therefore, even though Albania had not jointly agreed with Great Britain to submit the dispute to the Court, it was now bound to accept its decision.

It took the Court nearly another year and a half to hand down its decision, then seven more months to fix damages. Albania was held responsible for the damage and loss of life, and on December 15, 1949, Great Britain was granted compensation in the amount of £843,947.

As was mentioned above, this was the only instance where a defendant nation refused to accept a court decision, and the judgment was never paid. But Great Britain eventually collected part of it anyway in a rather devious manner. American occupation troops found some gold looted from Rome by the Nazis hidden in a salt mine in Germany. Italy claimed the gold, but Albania said it had originally come from Albania and belonged to that nation. The gold was turned over to Great Britain to hold until its ownership was established.

When an arbitrator decided the gold belonged to Albania, Great Britain simply kept it as part payment on the judgment against Albania.

THE TRUSTEESHIP COUNCIL

The Trusteeship Council is the least important organ of the United Nations because it is busily attempting to put itself out of business. At its fortieth session at U.N. headquarters in May and June of 1973, outgoing Council President W. Tapley Bennett, of the United States, said in his opening remarks that the Council was an example of a U.N. body that "has applied itself in a steady workmanlike way to obliterating itself."

What Mr. Bennett was referring to was that only two trust territories remain out of the original eleven, nine having now gained their independence. And the hope is that the last two will be brought to the point where they are capable of self-government within the next few years. When that happens, the Trusteeship Council will have no further function.

Before considering the Council, it is necessary to explain what trust territories are and how they came into being.

At the end of World War I some of the Allied nations wanted to divide up German colonies and the Ottoman Empire as spoils of war. They were opposed by President Woodrow Wilson in his famous Fourteen Points. Point Five called for ". . . impartial adjustment of all colonial claims, based upon . . . the principle that . . . the interests of the populations concerned must have equal weight with the equitable claims of the Government whose title is to be determined." Point Twelve said that Túrkey itself should retain its present boundaries, but the other nations under Turkish rule should be allowed self-determination.

It is popularly accepted that the lofty principles outlined in the Fourteen Points died amid the greed at Versailles. But actually, while the Versailles Treaty can hardly be said to embody the Fourteen Points, they did influence the negotiations. Point Fourteen, calling for "a general association of nations . . . for the purpose of affording mutual guarantees of political independence and territorial integrity to great and small states alike," resulted in the Covenant of the League of Nations. And Points Five and Twelve, although not incorporated in the treaty, resulted in a compromise.

The compromise was that the German colonies would be taken from Germany, and the Ottoman Empire would lose Syria and Lebanon, but no other nations would acquire them. Instead, each separate territory would be administered by one of the Allies under the supervision of the League of Nations. This was known as the mandate system.

The United Nations Charter set up a trusteeship system patterned after the League's mandate system. Article 77 of the Charter reads:

> 1. The trusteeship system shall apply to such territories in the following categories as may be placed thereunder by means of trusteeship agreements: ·
> (a) Territories now held under mandate;
> (b) Territories which may be detached from enemy states as a result of the second World War; and
> (c) Territories voluntarily placed under the system by states responsible for their administration.

Because there is a general impression that the League of Nations collapsed and disappeared with the outbreak of World War II in 1939, clause (a) may be a little puzzling. Actually, while the League certainly never accomplished much after 1939, it continued to exist until April 8, 1946, nearly ten months after the United Nations came into existence. On that date delegates held a final meeting to disband and to transfer its records and functions to the United Nations.

The U.N. Charter is full of references to League activities and functions that are now to be assumed by the United Nations. There was therefore a continuity of many activities that carried over from the League to the United Nations virtually without interruption, and, in some areas at least, something of a feeling that the United Nations was merely a continuation of the League. For instance, it is common practice for international lawyers to cite decisions of the Permanent Court of International Justice in the context that it is the same court as the present Court of International Justice.

The mandates were one of the carry-overs from the League. By the time the United Nations came into existence, Syria and Lebanon had become independent nations, but there were still seven mandates in Africa, Palestine was still a British mandate, and there were still three island mandates. Actually there were four, but Japan was the mandatory nation for the Caroline, Marshall, and Mariana islands, and her mandate became inoperative upon her defeat by the Allies in World War II. The United States, which had taken the islands, occupied them until decision could be made as to what to do with them.

Ten of the eleven mandates other than the Japanese one became trust territories under clause (a). Palestine was left in mandate status under the administration of Great Britain, that mandate ending on May 15, 1948. The Arab-Israeli War that instantly followed British withdrawal of its troops ended with Palestine divided three ways: into the State of Israel, the Hashemite Kingdom of Jordan, and the Gaza Strip, which is occupied by Egypt.

Some island possessions of Japan were taken from her under clause (b), were combined with the islands that had been under her mandate, and a total of 625 islands were made into a trusteeship now known as the Trust Territory of the Pacific Islands, or Micronesia, under the administration of the United States.

Clause (c) of Article 77 has never been applied. There have been suggestions from time to time that trouble spots such as Berlin and Jerusalem be placed under U.N. trusteeship by authority of this clause, but nothing has come to them.

The administrating nations of the trust territories are responsible to the Trusteeship Council. The Council in turn is responsible to the General Assembly in regard to all trust territories not classified as "strategic areas," and to the Security Council in regard to the latter. The distinction between the two types of trust territories was written into the U.N. Charter at the insistence of the United States, because it considered the Trust Territory of the Pacific Islands vital to the defense of Guam and Hawaii. That trust territory is the only one ever declared a strategic area.

The Trusteeship Council consists of three categories of members: one member from each nation administering a trust territory, one from each permanent member of the Security Council that is not the administrator of a trust territory, and as many other members elected to three-year terms by the General Assembly as will assure that the Council is equally divided between members who administer trust territories and members who do not.

When the Council was established in December, 1946, the eleven trusteeships were administered by the six nations of Australia, Belgium, France, New Zealand, the United Kingdom, and the United States. As permanent members of the Security Council not administering trusteeships, Nationalist China and the Soviet Union also had members on the Council. The General Assembly then had to elect four more members for three-year terms from other nations that were not administrators of trusteeships in order to bring the membership up to twelve.

In 1957 the number of trust territories was reduced to nine when Libya became a kingdom and British Togoland was absorbed into Ghana. Since then, seven more have attained independence, leaving only New Guinea, under the administration of Australia, and the Pacific Islands, under the administration of the United States.

This has had two rather odd effects. Because the Pacific Islands Trusteeship is classified as a strategic area and New Guinea is not, the Trusteeship Council is responsible to the Security Council for the former and to the General Assembly for the latter. The other oddity stems from the fact that although the U.N. Charter specifies that membership on the Council is to be equally divided between administrating and nonadministrating nations, it also specifies that all permanent members of the Security Council that are not administrators of trusteeships are to be represented. The result is that China, France, the United Kingdom, and the Soviet Union are all automatically members, which gives representation, in violation of the Charter, to twice as many nonadministering nations as to administering ones.

Cutting membership to four would violate the Charter in another way, though, so there is no way out of the dilemma other than amendment to the Charter, which seems unlikely because by the time ratification of two-thirds of the member nations was obtained, probably the Trusteeship Council would long since be no more.

The Council, in addition to receiving reports from the nations administering trust territories, is empowered to receive petitions from inhabitants of trust territories attesting to conditions or requesting reforms and to make inspections of territories to make sure they are being administered in the best interests of the inhabitants.

At the 1973 session of the Trusteeship Council it was reported that New Guinea may be ready for self-government by 1974. No specific date was offered as to when the Pacific Island Territory would be ready for independence, but since then tentative plans have been worked out for possible independence in 1976. Five of the six districts of the territory have accepted the plan, but it is currently held up because of a strong separatist movement on the part of the Mariana Island District, which would like to become a permanent commonwealth of the United States instead of a part of the new republic. This movement is largely motivated by economics, as commonwealth status would probably mean reversion of the Mariana island of Tinian back to a U.S. military base, with the attendant pouring of large sums of U.S. money into the area. (This is the island from which the planes that dropped atomic bombs on Japan took off.)

When New Guinea and the Territory of the Pacific Islands finally become independent, the Trusteeship Council will automatically expire.

THE SECRETARIAT

The Secretariat is the administrative organ of the United Nations, the one that does all the routine work necessary to make the organization function. The staff numbers nearly ten thousand employees. About one thousand work at the European office in Geneva, Switzerland, slightly more than a thousand are scattered around the world in various field assignments, the balance of approximately eight thousand work at U.N. Headquarters in New York City. These range from tour guides for the United Nations Building to international lawyers. Maintenance and clerical personnel are hired from the available employee market in New York City, with the result that most are American. But others are hired according to a system of national quotas that favors the smaller nations. Therefore the majority of higher-ranking employees are aliens.

The huge staff is divided into five offices and four departments. There are Offices of the Controller, of Personnel, of Legal Affairs, of General Services, and of Public Information. There are Departments of Economic and Social Affairs, of Conference Services, of Political and Security Council Affairs, and of Trusteeship and Non-Self-Governing Territories.

The Secretariat is administered by a secretary-general, who is elected by the General Assembly, on recommendation by the Security Council, for a term of five

years. The first Secretary-General was Norwegian states-
man Trygve Halvdan Lie, elected in February, 1946.
The present Secretary-General is the former U.N. representative to the General Assembly from Austria, Kurt
Waldheim.

The Secretary-General and his staff are expected to
be truly international in outlook and are forbidden by
the U.N. Charter to "seek or receive instruction from
any government or from any other authority external to
the organization." They are further exhorted to "refrain
from any action which might reflect on their position as
international officials responsible only to the organization."

In addition to the Secretary-General's purely administrative duties, Article 99 of the U.N. Charter states that
he "may bring to the attention of the Security Council
any matter which in his opinion may threaten the maintenance of international peace and security."

This article has caused some controversy between the
Western nations and the communist countries. The former interpret it as requiring a certain element of leadership from the Secretary-General in the formulation of
policies designed to assure peace. The latter insist that
he has no such power and, in effect, is merely the head
clerk of the organization.

The present Secretary-General interprets his main
task as one of leadership toward permanent international peace and security, and in pursuing that goal he has
been somewhat more outspoken than previous Secretar-
ies-General, a trait that has brought him both commen-
dation and condemnation from the world's press. In a
speech in Oslo, Norway, on May 10, 1973, Mr.
Waldheim wryly took note of this by quoting the first Secretary-General, Trygve Lie, as once characterizing the office as "the most impossible job in the world."

Chapter IV

REGIONAL INTERNATIONAL ORGANIZATIONS

There are more than two thousand organizations that can be classified as international organizations. Most of these are privately sponsored (e.g., the International Committee of the Red Cross) rather than being associations of sovereign nations, but somewhere between three hundred and four hundred *are* intergovernmental organizations created by multilateral treaties.

The majority of these are of a technical nature, designed to facilitate cooperation in such matters as postal regulations and weather-gathering information. There are a lesser number that can be classified as primarily political organizations. Among these are a number of regional international organizations. These may be roughly divided into three types: mutual defense pacts; organizations concerned both with mutual defense and with other matters, such as the peaceful settlement of disputes among members or facilitating trade and cultural exchange; organizations concerned solely with cooperation among members in nondefense matters.

Since in most cases all the members of these regional organizations are also members of the United Nations, cooperation between them and the United Nations is automatically provided for in the U.N. Charter.

Article 52 of the Charter says, "The Security Council shall encourage the development of pacific settlement of local disputes through such regional arrangements . . ." but also specifies, "This Article in no way impairs the application of Articles 34 and 35." Article 34 empowers the Security Council to investigate any dispute threatening peace, and Article 35 stipulates that any nation may bring such disputes to its attention.

In brief, regional organizations may launder their own dirty linen if they are capable of doing so, but if a dispute threatens to get out of hand, the United Nations may step in at any time it chooses to. The U.N. Charter further provides that no enforcement action may be taken by regional organizations without the approval of the Security Council.

The more important mutual defense pacts are the North Atlantic Treaty Organization, the Warsaw Treaty Organization, and the Southeast Asia Treaty Organization.

NORTH ATLANTIC TREATY ORGANIZATION (NATO)

Signed at Washington, D.C., on April 4, 1949, this multilateral treaty decrees that an attack on any member is an attack on all, and requires all members to come to the assistance of an attacked member. The implication of the treaty is that "assistance" means military assistance, but the actual wording is that assistance shall be given by each member nation by "such action as it deems necessary." This leaves an escape clause that would allow a member nation merely to make diplomatic protest instead of furnishing military assistance to an attacked member, but actually this is not too important. Although the treaty doesn't specifically mention from whom attack might be expected, essentially it is a defensive alliance against the Soviet Union and its allies. U.S. military power provides its main teeth, and regardless of how the treaty reads, the member nations are likely to follow whatever lead the United States takes. This factor will be elaborated on in the next chapter.

Originally there were twelve members of NATO, but Greece, Turkey, and the German Federal Republic subsequently joined by accession, bringing the present number to fifteen. All are European nations except Canada, Iceland, and the United States.

The organizational structure of NATO is rather elaborate. The policy-making body is the North Atlantic Council, which is alternately composed of two different types of membership. An ambassador is appointed from each member nation as a permanent representative, and this group meets on a regular basis at least once a week. But once or twice a year the foreign ministers, or, in some cases, the heads of state, meet together and replace the permanent representatives as the Council. The Council is chaired by a secretary-general of NATO, who is always one of the member nation's foreign ministers. The office is rotated from nation to nation in alphabetical order.

NATO is not merely an alliance, but is also a military organization, with a permanent military force stationed in four sections of Europe, which is furnished on a quota basis by all the member nations except Iceland. (Iceland has no military force.) NATO forces are under the Military Committee, composed of the chiefs of staff from fourteen nations and a civilian representative from Iceland. Supreme Headquarters, Allied Powers in Europe (SHAPE) is located in Belgium.

Although NATO is primarily a military alliance, the North Atlantic Council in 1956 voted to authorize the Secretary-General to initiate inquiries into disputes between member nations, with their consent, and to set up negotiation procedures to settle them. Since then, several disputes among member nations—notably the settlement in 1959 of a disagreement between Greece, Turkey, and the United Kingdom over the island of Cyprus —have been settled by this procedure without having to be referred to the United Nations.

WARSAW TREATY ORGANIZATION

The so-called Warsaw Pact came about as a direct result of the admission of West Germany to NATO. Signed at Warsaw, Poland, on May 14, 1955, it followed that admission by only two weeks.

There were in force at that time a number of bilateral and multilateral treaties of mutual defense among the Soviet Union and the other eight communist nations of Europe. For the most part these were motivated by the assumed threat of possible attack by the Western powers, and some had come about in direct reaction to NATO. The admission to NATO of West Germany, of which the Soviet Union has always been apprehensive, decided the Soviet leadership (at that time divided between Nikita Khrushchev and Nikolai Bulganin) to consolidate and codify these various treaties into a single multilateral agreement. That agreement, which came to be called the Warsaw Pact, was agreed by the signatories to last for twenty years, which means it will expire in 1975 unless extended by amendment.

The Soviet Union and seven of the other eight communist nations of Europe were signatories to the pact. Yugoslavia refused to sign. Albania formally withdrew in 1968, leaving only six nations aside from the Soviet Union.

The Warsaw Treaty Organization is essentially a military alliance and, like NATO, provides for a standing army furnished by the member nations on a quota basis. U.S. intelligence estimates that force at about 4.5 million troops, roughly three-fourths of them Soviet troops.

While there is some flowery wordage in the treaty pledging the signatories to abstain from violence, or even the threat of violence, in relations with other nations, there are no specific procedures laid down for the settlement of disputes between members. The reason for this became apparent after the treaty had been in force only a little over a year. One of the provisions of the treaty permitted Soviet troops to be stationed in all member nations. The crushing of the Hungarian uprising in 1956 demonstrated why the Soviet Union had not felt it necessary to include any procedures in the pact for the peaceable settlement of disputes among members: the Soviet Union obviously intended to supervise the internal affairs of the satellites so closely that disputes would not erupt.

Because the Warsaw Pact is as much a tool of Soviet domination over the pact nations as it is a mutual defense alliance, it has had a much more stormy existence than NATO. Shortly before the Hungarian Revolution, a similar uprising took place in Poland, also triggered by resentment at Soviet interference in local affairs. Less bloody than Hungary's, largely because the Polish Government managed to suppress it without Soviet help, it resulted in the withdrawal of Soviet occupation troops from Poland as a conciliatory gesture of the Polish people. Then came the Hungarian Revolution, the withdrawal of Albania from the pact in 1968, and the Czechoslovakian uprising the same year. While all the original signatories except Albania remain in the organization, unrest in the satellite nations because of Soviet involvement in internal affairs may well result in amendments allowing much more autonomy by member nations if the pact is renewed in 1975.

Southeast Asia Treaty Organization (SEATO)

SEATO was created by the Southeast Asia Collective Defense Treaty of September 8, 1954, signed at Manila by Australia, France, New Zealand, Pakistan, the Philippines, Thailand, the United Kingdom, and the United States. Its specific purpose is to prevent further communist expansion in Southeast Asia and in the Southwest Pacific. While the treaty calls for mutual defense in case of attack, without specifying that the attack must be by a communist nation, the United States ratification was accompanied by an "Understanding and Interpretation" committing the United States only in the event of communist attack.

(In the United States a treaty must be either ratified as is by the Senate or rejected. It may not be amended. However the Senate may add an Understanding and Interpretation of its meaning which, if it differs from what the framers meant, in effect constitutes an amendment because the United States is committed to observe the treaty only within its own understanding and interpretation. Other nations have this same privilege, of course.)

SEATO differs from most defensive alliances on two scores. First, its most powerful members—France, the United States, and the United Kingdom—are not geographically part of the area guaranteed defense against attack, but are parties to it merely to protect their interests in the area. Second, a number of the most important nations within the defense area are not party to the treaty. India, Burma, and Ceylon have refused participation because of a continuing foreign policy of nonalignment with either the communist powers or the anticommunist bloc. South Vietnam, Cambodia, and Laos, although guaranteed against attack under the treaty, were never asked to join for some rather complicated reasons having to do with the provisions of the 1954 cease-fire agreement between France and North Vietnam. The result is that the nations comprising the major portion of the defense area are guaranteed defense against communist aggression without having committed themselves to any action in the event of attack on a member state.

SEATO, unlike NATO and the Warsaw Treaty Organization, has no standing military force, but relies on the mobile strike forces of its members, which regularly engage in maneuvers in the area.

SEATO is directed by a council consisting of representatives of the member nations, chaired by a secretary-general. The permanent headquarters is at Bangkok, Thailand. The treaty makes no provisions for peaceable settlement of disputes between member nations, but nevertheless is slightly more than a mere regional defense pact. There is an Economic Committee under the Council that conducts an agricultural research program designed to improve the agricultural output of the entire region.

SEATO's greatest test to date, the war in Vietnam, has not been a fair one because of a disagreement among the member nations on the vital question of whether that was a war of aggression or a civil war. With two of the three most powerful members, France and the United Kingdom, disagreeing with the United States position that it was a war of aggression, SEATO sat that out as an organization and let its members take what individual action they chose to.

The more important regional organizations created both for mutual defense and for other purposes are the Organization of American States, the Arab League, and the Organization of African Unity.

ORGANIZATION OF AMERICAN STATES (OAS)

In 1889 representatives of North American, Central American, and South American nations met at Washington, D.C., to form the International Union of American Republics. Initially the union was solely concerned with facilitating trade. In 1910, after a number of similar conferences that expanded the purposes of the union into such matters as compulsory arbitration of disputes, patents and copyrights, and the naturalization of citizens, the word "international" was dropped from the name, and it became simply the Union of American Republics. On April 30, 1948, the members signed a treaty at Bogotá, Colombia, to go into effect in December, 1951, converting the union to the Organization of American States and giving it a charter. Twenty-four nations, including the United States, are members of the OAS.

The OAS Charter states that it "reaffirms" the principles already established by treaties, resolutions, and proclamations under the organization's previous two names, and therefore the Charter amounts more to a codification of existing practice than to the establishment of any new principles. The primary aims of the OAS are to provide machinery for the peaceful settlement of disputes among the members and for military and economic cooperation among them. The Charter provides for mutual assistance in the event of armed attack from outside the OAS and for procedures to preserve peace among the member nations. A two-thirds vote binds members to whatever peace-keeping action is decided upon (subject to approval by the U.N. Security Council, of course), including military action, but no member may be required to furnish military assistance against its wishes.

The policy-making and decision-making body of the OAS is the Council, which sits in Washington, D.C., and consists of a U.S. representative, plus the ambassadors to the United States of the other member nations. The Council is chaired by a secretary-general, elected by the Council for a ten-year term. The Council deals with emergency matters as they arise and also handles any other matters of concern to the member nations.

Under the Council is an Advisory Defense Committee composed of military officers of the member nations. Its function is to advise the Council concerning military matters when the OAS contemplates military action to cope with any situation threatening a member nation.

The Pan American Union is the OAS's equivalent of the U.N. Secretariat. It is the administrative body that does all the paper work and handles other administrative chores.

The Arab League

In 1945 there were only seven independent Arab nations. Yemen, with the longest period of independence, had been granted autonomy by Turkey in 1913. Egypt, which had long been under British control, although supposedly an independent kingdom, had gained real independence in 1922. The other five, which had been League of Nations mandates under either France or Great Britain, had gained their independence at various times from 1919 to 1944.

On March 22, 1945, these seven nations signed a pact at Cairo creating the League of Arab States. Since then, eleven other Arab nations that have subsequently gained their independence have joined the league by accession, bringing the present membership to eighteen.

The stated aims of the pact were "to strengthen the ties between the participant states, to coordinate their political program in such a way as to effect real collaboration between them, to preserve their independence and sovereignty and to consider in general the affairs and interests of the Arab countries." Members were pledged not to use force against each other in the event of disputes. In case of attack from outside the league on any member, the Council was to meet in immediate emergency session to decide what action to take.

Agreement merely to meet and discuss the matter in case of attack against a member nation made the league considerably less than a military alliance. However, in 1950 a Joint Defense and Economic Cooperation Treaty was executed by the league members which declared the same principle embodied in NATO: that an attack on any member would be considered an attack upon all. While this was a separate treaty, and not an amendment to the original Cairo agreement, the same nations are party to both. Therefore, while technically speaking the Arab League is not in itself a mutual defense organization, the members are bound by this separate treaty to come to each other's assistance in the event of attack from outside the league.

The chief organ of the league is a council composed of one representative from each member nation, each with equal vote. The Council meets only twice a year, unless an emergency session is called, and its power is considerably weakened by a provision in the league pact that its decisions are binding only if unanimously reached, which in effect gives all members veto power. There is a permanent secretariat located in Cairo, headed by a secretary-general who is appointed by the Council for an indefinite term. Several subcouncils and committees under the Council are concerned with economic, social, and cultural matters.

Disagreements among the member nations have made the league fall far short of the vision of Arab unity that initially inspired it. Shortly after the formation of the league, five of the original seven nations helped draft the U.N. Charter at San Francisco. Their representatives announced to the U.N. delegates that they considered themselves first representatives of the Arab League and only secondarily representatives of their own nations, and therefore could be counted on to vote as a bloc in the General Assembly. That solidarity quickly evaporated, not only in the General Assembly but in their own regional relationships.

The first test of league solidarity came in 1948, when it attempted to prevent the establishment of the State of Israel in Palestine. With all the might of the Arab world directed at tiny Israel, they were driven back, largely because they lacked unity of purpose and coordination of effort. The Israeli forces, on the other hand, were highly coordinated and were single-minded in purpose: they were fighting for their very existence.

The basic factor of disagreement among the Arab nations is that there is no concerted foreign policy. Some Arab nations are friendly to the West, some to the communist bloc, and some insist on strict neutrality. Divisive forces in the Arab world have continued to make the Arab League ineffective in every crisis except the Suez crisis of 1956, when for the first and only time the league presented a united front to the world. Details of that crisis are described in the next chapter.

In areas other than political the league has been more successful. An Economic Council under the League Council has improved trade between the various Arab nations. A Boycott Office has had some success in organizing an economic boycott of Israel. And an annual Petroleum Conference has helped solve some of the problems of oil-rich but industrially impoverished Arab nations.

ORGANIZATION OF AFRICAN UNITY (OAU)

The OAU Charter was signed by thirty-two African nations at Addis Ababa, Ethiopia, on May 24, 1963. Since then, nine more nations have joined by accession, to bring the present membership to forty-one.

In general the OAU has three aims. One is to promote the unity of Africa by coordinating the economic and foreign policies of the member nations on a basis of strict nonalignment. This means that insofar as possible the members will operate in economic areas and in foreign affairs as a neutral bloc, aligning with neither the communist world nor the Western powers, but acting solely in the self-interest of Africa. The second aim is to defend the independence and sovereignty of members. The third is to assist those areas of Africa still under foreign domination to be granted self-determination.

The chief policy-making body of OAU is the Conference of Heads of State, but since this meets only every two years, a Council of Ministers carries on business between summit meetings. This is composed of foreign ministers of the member nations and meets twice a year. The administrative agency of the organization is a secretariat located at Addis Ababa, headed by a secretary-general.

There are a number of committees under the Council, two of which are particularly important. All disputes between members are required under the Charter to be submitted to the Commission of Mediation, Conciliation, and Arbitration. Members have not always observed this clause, with the result that there have been some armed clashes among members, but there have also been some successful mediations by the commission. During the 1960s, for example, the commission successfully mediated three major boundary disputes (Algeria versus Morocco, the Somali Republic versus Ethiopia, and the Somali Republic versus Kenya) and also arranged the evacuation of mercenaries from the Congo in 1967. The National Liberation Committee (NLC) actively works to assist areas the OAU considers still not free from colonialism to attain full independence. Although technically an independent nation, the Republic of South Africa (known as the Union of South Africa until 1961) is considered one such area by the OAU because of its domination of the predominantly black population by a white minority which originally was largely Dutch. Southern Rhodesia is a second such area, and Portugal still has some colonial possessions in Africa. The NLC conducts a heavy propaganda and diplomatic campaign against the oppressive policies of all three nations in the United Nations General Assembly and in the international press in an attempt to force the three to grant self-determination to the peoples of the areas they dominate.

Regional organizations concerned solely with cooperation between nations on nondefensive matters include the Council of Europe, the European Coal and Steel Community, the European Economic Community, and the European Atomic Energy Community.

COUNCIL OF EUROPE

An organization created by a convention signed at London in May, 1949, by ten European nations, the purpose of the Council of Europe is to promote cultural exchange and to coordinate economic and social interests. While the organization has only advisory powers, it has brought about a number of multilateral treaties involving social and cultural matters. Its most notable achievement has been the European Convention on Human Rights, signed at Rome November 4, 1950, which laid down a bill of rights for the signatories' nationals. Rights include guarantees against torture or inhuman treatment, slavery and servitude, and the positive guarantees of "liberty and security of person," freedom of thought, religion, association, and expression.

The council is organized into a Committee of Ministers, which is the body that makes recommendations to the member nations, and a Consultive Assembly under the Committee of Ministers.

EUROPEAN COAL AND STEEL COMMUNITY (ECSC)

The treaty establishing the ECSC was signed at Paris on April 18, 1951, by six European nations—Belgium, France, the German Federal Republic, Italy, Luxemburg, and the Netherlands. Its immediate purpose was to establish a common market for coal and steel among the member nations by abolishing customs duties and other restrictions on the free movement between nations of products related to those two industries. Its ultimate purpose was to work toward a United States of Europe, to be attained on a gradual basis by similar treaties of cooperation.

The nine-member High Authority of the ECSC was unique among international bodies in that its decisions were binding upon the member nations. Of course its decisions were limited to matters affecting the marketing of coal and steel, but nevertheless it represented the first instance in which nations willingly surrendered part of their absolute sovereignty unconditionally to an international body.

Beneath the High Authority was a Common Assembly of seventy-eight members, a Special Council of Ministers, and a Court of Justice. The latter was solely a court of appeals for nations wishing to appeal adverse decisions by the High Authority.

European Economic Community (EEC or Common Market) European Atomic Energy Community (Euratom)

The European Economic Community and the European Atomic Energy Community are lumped together for reasons that will become obvious. Signed at Rome on March 25, 1957, by the six member nations of the ECSC, the Common Market Treaty was the next step in the eventual goal of creating a United States of Europe. It established free trade for all goods among member nations and also provided for the free movement of both capital and persons between nations. For persons born and raised in the United States, the significance of the latter two items may be difficult to comprehend, for we live in a nation where both the freedom to invest money in any state, regardless of where you live, and freedom of movement between the fifty individual states is accepted as a matter of course. But in Europe there were all sorts of restrictions on how much money could be taken out of the various nations or could be invested in foreign nations, and a visa was required every time you wanted to cross a border.

The EEC was originally organized under a nine-member commission similar to the High Authority of the ECSC.

At the time the Common Market Treaty was signed, the same six nations signed a treaty establishing the European Atomic Energy Community, whose purpose was to coordinate the research and development of atomic energy for peaceful uses. The chief policy-making organ of Euratom was a five-member commission.

In July, 1967, the ECSC High Authority and the commissions of the other two communities were replaced by a single European Commission to administratively supervise all three. The Common Assembly of the ECSC was increased to a membership of 142, was renamed the European Parliament, and was given the authority to make recommendations concerning all three communities. The ECSC Special Council of Ministers became simply the Council of Ministers and was elevated over the European Commission as the chief policy-making body for all three communities. The Court of Justice is now shared by all three also.

Nevertheless, while having common membership and sharing common administrative organs, the ECSC, the EEC, and Euratom are still legally three separate regional organizations.

On January 1, 1973, Great Britain, Ireland, and Denmark were admitted to the Common Market, increasing its present membership to nine.

Chapter V

WHY INTERNATIONAL
LAW WORKS

Several years ago on a network television show former Israeli Ambassador to the United States Abba Eban
(now Israel's foreign minister) defined international law
as "the law which the wicked do not obey and which the
righteous do not enforce."

Fortunately most of the world's diplomats do not
share Mr. Eban's skepticism about the effectiveness of
international law. But among the average citizens of all
nations there is widespread doubt that it amounts to
much more than useless rhetoric which the diplomats of
the various nations direct at each other during U.N. de-
bates.

People remember such incidents as Russia's 1956
invasion of Hungary and its 1968 invasion of Czechoslovakia, when in each instance the Security Council of the
United Nations was still debating as those nations were
crushed into submission by Soviet troops. On both occa-
sions there was general outrage in the United States, both
against Russia for its action and against the United Nations for its inaction. More recently the United States
has been on the receiving end of public outrage in other
nations for our military actions in Indochina over a period of more than ten years, which finally ended on August 15, 1973. As in the case of Russia, the only action
taken against the United States by the United Nations
during that entire ten years was debate.

All three instances seem to substantiate the common
charge that international law is meaningless when one of
the superpowers decides to ignore it. It should be understood, though, that both the Soviet Union and the Unit-

ed States *claimed* to be operating within the rules of international law in all three cases.

In the first instance Russia claimed that its invasion of Hungary was merely to restore order and was at the request of the "legal" Hungarian Government. Actually what happened was that the original uprising in Hungary was both against the puppet Hungarian Government and the occupation forces of Russia. In an attempt to pacify the revolutionists the Soviet Union approved the appointment as Premier of the popular Imre Nagy, who had been ousted from that office the previous year because of his liberal views, and withdrew all Russian occupation troops from the nation. But the moment Nagy started to form a coalition government, including some non-Communists, Russia sent troops back in. After Hungary was crushed and a new "revolutionary peasant-worker" government was formed under puppet premier János Kadar, Nagy's government was declared illegal, and Nagy himself was executed as a traitor. But at the time of the invasion it was clearly the legal government and had been recognized as such by Russia.

In the second instance, the 1968 invasion of Czechoslovakia, Russia was on even shakier legal grounds when it attempted to justify the invasion under the doctrine of *spheres of influence*. Under this doctrine a major power declares its right to defend smaller powers within its sphere of influence against outside attack. This has generally been accepted as compatible with customary international law. However, interference in internal affairs is generally regarded as illegal, and in this case there was no attack from outside. Soviet representative on the Security Council Yakov Malik attempted to manufacture one, though, when he claimed in a speech before the Security Council that troops of the Soviet Union and its allies had entered Czechoslovakia at the request of its government because of the "threat created by foreign and domestic reaction to its socialist and constitutional state system." The implication seemed to be that the uprising against the communist regime had somehow been brought about by foreign agents who had infiltrated the country, and that this constituted "invasion."

In the third instance, the United States claim that its intervention in South Vietnam was legally justifiable under international law is more defensible, but there is still room for considerable difference of opinion. The so-called Iron Curtain countries have consistently argued that the National Liberation Front (more popularly known as the Vietcong) represents a spontaneous internal revolt, and therefore the disturbance in South Vietnam was, and still is, a civil war. The United States has always insisted that the Vietcong is a subversive organization ruled by North Vietnam, and therefore amounts to invasion by an enemy force—a claim similar to Mr. Malik's justification for the invasion of Czechoslovakia, but with somewhat more substance. No one, including the Soviet Union, ever denied that there was an actual Vietcong, so that the argument hinged merely on what it was: a revolutionary group or an invasion force. The shadowy foreign agents Mr. Malik claimed had infiltrated Czechoslovakia never appeared anywhere other than in his speech, however.

There is widespread sentiment, even in the United States, that regardless of the legal niceties, our involvement in Indochina was immoral. But we are concerned here only with legal aspects, and even the most vehement opponents of our involvement have had to depend more on rhetoric than on legal arguments in their charge that the United States deliberately violated international law. We *may* have, but there is no clear-cut legal evidence of it.

At the time of both the Hungarian and the Czechoslovakian invasions draft resolutions were introduced in the Security Council condemning the invasions, calling for the withdrawal of the invasion forces, and calling upon all members of the United Nations to bring diplomatic pressure on the Soviet Union to abide by the resolutions. Because of the veto power, neither resolution passed, the Soviet Union, quite naturally, casting its vote against them.

Despite the defeat of these resolutions because of Russia's veto and despite worldwide outrage at Russia's actions in both cases, there is no incontrovertible proof that either was a deliberate violation of international law. Most authorities on international law in noncommunist countries regard them as clearly illegal, but most authorities in communist countries are just as firm in the opinion that they were legal.

The point is that in neither of the instances involving the Soviet Union, nor in the case of United States involvement in Indochina, did the superpowers in question simply disregard international law, but rather made every effort to justify their actions under its principles. Even though the arguments in all three cases may be suspect, it is clear that both nations are sensitive enough to world opinion to feel compelled to defend their actions as legal. And this sensitivity to world opinion is one of the most powerful enforcement tools in international law.

There is a widespread impression in this hemisphere and in Western Europe that the communist nations ignore or repudiate treaties whenever their self-interest conflicts with their treaty obligations. There has been a tendency, particularly in the United States, to draw self-righteous comparisons between our own exemplary international behavior and the lawlessness of the Soviet Union. Prior to the Nixon administration policy of improving relations with the communist nations, the U.S. Department of State, for instance, had a policy of periodically publishing lists in its *Department of State Bulletin* of treaty violations by the Soviet Union since the communist revolution of 1917. There has been a marked lack of such lists since the Cold War thaw, and since the June, 1973, visit to the United States of Leonid Brezhnev, general secretary of the Central Committee of the Communist party of the Soviet Union, it seems extremely unlikely that any more will appear in the near future, that visit having ended on a note of such cordial friendliness between Mr. Brezhnev and President Nixon.

Before the thaw in the Cold War the Western world was just as regularly accused of treaty violations by the communist nations. The fact is that mutual charges of treaty violations by nations go back into the dim reaches of history. And a disinterested observer might find it difficult to decide whether the Western nations or the Soviet bloc practices international relations on the higher moral plane.

One difficulty is that the rules of international law, like all laws, are subject to different interpretation. When you consider that in the United States the Supreme Court seldom hands down a unanimous decision, and frequently there is a 5–4 split, it is not surprising that there is frequent divergence of opinion in international law. But a Supreme Court decision, even if split, decides that issue beyond further argument insofar as the municipal law of the United States is concerned. There is no international tribunal with the equivalent power to "make" international law. The International Court of Justice or international arbitrators often hand down decisions that have the force of law, but as has been previously pointed out, there is no way to force a sovereign nation to accept the jurisdiction of either the Court or an arbitrator against its desires. Therefore some disputes simply remain unresolved, with both sides claiming to be in the right.

There have, of course, been deliberate and blatant violations of treaties throughout history. The United States record for treaty violations with the Indian nations, for instance, is very nearly 100 percent. Furthermore, we have the distinction of having violated the first two treaties we ever negotiated, the Treaty of Amity and Commerce and the Treaty of Alliance, both made with France in 1778. The latter was violated first, when President George Washington, with the concurrence of his Cabinet, which included both Thomas Jefferson and Alexander Hamilton, issued a proclamation of neutrality at the outbreak of war between France and England in 1793. This was a deliberate treaty violation, because the treaty required us to declare war against England if England warred against France. The proclamation of neutrality was in the best interest of the United States, because we ran a grave risk of losing our independence back to England if we went to war at that point, but nevertheless three of our founding fathers that schoolchildren in America are taught to look up to as towers of personal integrity jointly agreed to the deliberate violation of our first political treaty.

The following year the Jay Treaty of 1794, also previously mentioned, shattered the Treaty of Amity and Commerce with France by making concessions to England in direct violation of the French treaty.

In an interesting book titled *The Treaty Trap*, by Laurence W. Beilenson, the author covers the history of nearly a thousand broken treaties, from a 1535 treaty between France and Turkey up to the year 1968.

Despite all these discouraging statistics, the fact is that virtually all nations make every attempt to operate within the rules of international law, and it is broken much less regularly than the municipal law of most nations. In the United States, for example, nearly a half million people are charged with serious crimes each year, and about half are convicted.

If war is taken as the supreme example of the breakdown of international law, consider that in the history of the entire world civil wars and rebellions have greatly outnumbered international wars. For instance, over the past four thousand years China has engaged in no more than a half-dozen international wars, but has had something like forty revolutions. Many Central and South American nations can boast an even larger ratio of civil wars to international wars.

In *The Treaty Trap* Beilenson quite convincingly makes the point that throughout history all nations, regardless of their types of government, have broken political treaties when it was to their selfish interest to do so. But please note that his study is concerned almost entirely with *political* treaties.

Political treaties are lawmaking treaties, but this does not mean that lawmaking treaties are necessarily political treaties. There are several types of political treaties, but they have in common the factor that their primary purpose is to reinforce national security. Thus a mutual defense pact is a political treaty, whereas an extradition treaty is not, although both are lawmaking treaties.

In addition to alliances, in which the signatories

pledge to aid each other in the event of war, political treaties may include such agreements as:

1. Disarmament treaties, in which the signatories agree either to reduce or limit their arms. The 1973 agreement between the United States and the Soviet Union to limit strategic nuclear weapons falls in this category.

2. Economic sanctions treaties, in which allies pledge to shut off trade with a third nation in order to force the third nation through economic pressure to agree to some desired course of action.

3. Guarantee treaties, in which nations guarantee the territorial integrity or political independence of other nations. This type of treaty has been the basis of most of our involvement in Indochina.

4. Peace treaties, in which territories are divided and spheres of influence are fixed by the victors, and terms of defeat are imposed on the losers.

5. Settlement treaties, in which the same matters that are usually negotiated in peace treaties are settled by negotiation without war.

6. Subsidy treaties, in which one ally promises another to pay the cost of maintaining its armed forces, as the United States did for the Soviet Union during World War II. Russia furnished the manpower for the eastern front against the Axis powers, but the arms and equipment were furnished almost entirely by the United States. A subsidy treaty may also involve a guarantee to pay an ally to remain neutral in the event of war. The Marshall Plan could be considered a sophisticated version of that type of treaty. While it exacted no political commitments in return for economic aid, its effect was to create a bloc of nations friendly to the United States, so that the charge by Marshall Plan critics that it was merely a device for "buying" friendships had at least some basis in fact.

Quite obviously the violation of a political treaty is likely to have much more serious international consequences than the violation of a nonpolitical one. Wars, although not necessarily brought about by the violation of political treaties, almost without exception involve the breaking of such treaties. If the world is ever destroyed by a nuclear holocaust, the breaking of political treaties will have to precede the destruction.

But the very possibility of that happening has tended to make the violation of political treaties increasingly less common. Of the nearly one thousand treaty violations listed in *The Treaty Trap*, only eighty-five were signed since the creation of the United Nations. This is not to say that only eighty-five treaties were broken during the twenty-three-year period involved, because the list includes only the political treaties broken and only the political treaties whose violations had serious international consequences. Nevertheless, the number of treaty violations is a decided improvement over previous ages.

The reason for this has nothing to do with an improvement in human nature. Modern warfare simply involves too great risk and too little potential profit for nations to plunge into it with the same casualness common in previous times. Blatant wars of conquest simply to acquire new territory are things of the past. The cost of modern warfare, in terms of both human life and resources, has become so enormous that there is general agreement that no nation any longer can "win" a war, but there can be only degrees of loss.

There still are what have become known as "contained wars," of course, when nations decide their national interests are worth the risks. And the threat of World War III still hovers. In the August, 1973, *Reader's Digest* commentator Joseph Alsop rather chillingly placed the odds of a nuclear attack on Communist China by the Soviet Union during the next three years at one in four. But in the field of international relations there is a tendency to regard a World War III as unthinkable, not through any ostrichlike avoidance of the obvious, but because it *is* unthinkable. Almost certainly a third world war between the superpowers would be a nuclear war, and the consensus is that if such a war did not reduce this globe to an uninhabitable cinder, the destruction would be so vast that what little humanity was left would be thrown back into another period of Dark

Ages. Since there would be no point in attempting to plan contingencies on either basis, the only reasonable philosophy is to rely on international law to prevent World War III from ever beginning.

Fortunately, in the main, international law does work. The widespread impression that it is more or less constantly violated stems from two factors. First, only violations of the law receive public attention through the news media. It is not "news" that since 1848 the United States had not had a dispute with either of the nations bordering it that was not peaceably settled under the rules of international law. It *is* news when our government does something as legally suspect as training and financing a rebel force of exiled Cubans to invade Cuba.

With the United States alone having something like four thousand treaties in effect, the worldwide total of treaties in force among all nations is incalculable. Most of these are never violated. It is only the few that are violated that come to public attention.

The second factor is that people tend to confuse international dispute with the breaking of international law, assuming that a dispute must mean that one party or the other has violated the law. But just as two individuals can have a legal dispute in a court of civil law without either being guilty of any crime, so can nations disagree without either violating international law.

For instance, a dispute may stem from disagreement as to fact. The communist nations insist the Vietnam War is a civil war; the United States insists it is a war of aggression against South Vietnam by North Vietnam. Or there may be disagreement as to what the law is in a particular instance. Some of the less-developed nations have declared their legal right to confiscate and nationalize industries owned by foreigners without paying compensation; the developed nations, whose citizen-investors would tend to be the losers in such circumstances, totally disagree. There are defensible arguments on both sides.

Having established the premise that international law does work most of the time, at least as well, and perhaps even better than, some systems of municipal law, we are

ready to examine what makes it work. Obviously the
sanctions used to enforce municipal law are unworkable
in international law. You cannot fine or jail a nation for
violating the law. Consequently the factors that help to
enforce international law are quite different from those
employed to enforce municipal law:

SELF-INTEREST

The absence of an international legislature is a strengthening rather than a weakening factor in international
law, simply because it assures a system of rules at least
generally palatable to the different nations. Because
they create the law themselves instead of having it thrust
upon them by a lawmaking body, nations obviously are
going to create laws they regard as to their own interests, and therefore are not likely to risk destroying such
laws by breaking them. While it is possible for a nation
to be forced to accept a rule it dislikes through pressures
of various sorts, or that its interests may change after accepting a rule, the principle holds in general.

The interdependence of nations in international trade
makes it to the self-interest of all nations to agree on
many rules of international law. But there are also may
other areas where international cooperation is to the
benefit of all nations. For instance, all nations have a
selfish interest in ecological matters such as the preser-
vation of resources and the avoidance of polluting the
oceans. Rules to accomplish such ends are best laid
down in treaty form. Also, in recurrent problems such
as the right to fly aircraft over the airspace of foreign
nations, it is to everyone's interest to have specific rules
agreed to, simply to avoid a new dispute in every case.

THE DANGER OF PRECEDENT

A nation that breaks a rule of customary law may find
itself in the position at some future date of having the
precedent thrown back into its face. As an example, in

1961 India invaded Goa, defending its action on the grounds that Portugal had originally taken the area from India by force, and India was merely taking it back. Since Portugal had held Goa from 1504, the argument was hardly a strong one. Nevertheless, the international community eventually accepted it, although somewhat reluctantly.

A year later Communist China invaded some areas in the Himalaya Mountains belonging to India on the grounds that India had inherited them from Great Britain when she gained her independence, and Great Britain had originally taken them from China. India's protest brought the bland reply from China that she was merely applying the same rule that India had invoked to justify her invasion of Goa.

India was placed in the embarrassing position of being unable to charge China with a violation of international law without admitting a similar violation herself. The possibility of this occurring is often a deterrent to breaking the international law, because there is a general tendency among diplomats to weigh very carefully the long-range disadvantages of breaking a particular rule of international law against whatever the immediate advantages may be.

WORLD OPINION

World opinion is a larger factor in the enforcement of international law than most people realize. A nation's reputation for keeping its promises is vital to its foreign policy for reasons far more important than the mere desire to look well in the eyes of the world. Failure to keep its promises can result in severe diplomatic setbacks all out of proportion to the immediate gain.

As a case in point, the 1968 invasion of Czechoslovakia by the Soviet Union and its Warsaw Pact allies resulted in the Nuclear Weapons Non-Proliferation Treaty of July 1, 1968, not being ratified by West Germany. It very nearly was not ratified by the United States either, despite the United States and the Soviet Union being its principal drafters. Several U.S. Senators publicly opposed ratification on the grounds that it was pointless to enter into treaty arrangements with a nation that blatantly violated treaties. It was finally ratified and went into effect for the United States on March 5, 1970. It has still not been ratified by West Germany, however, although seventy-four other nations in addition to the United States and the Soviet Union are now party to it. This was a major setback to Russian foreign policy, because the Soviet Union had long been concerned with preventing the spread of nuclear weapons to nations not already possessing them, and was particularly fearful of West Germany.

NATO is an example of how a good reputation for honoring commitments aids a nation's foreign policy. Under the terms of this alliance the United States guarantees to defend its European allies in the event of attack by Russia. If either the Soviet Union or the European members of NATO felt there was a strong chance that the United States would not keep its commitment in the event of Soviet attack, the alliance would no doubt fall apart. But despite the fact that the treaty-keeping record of the United States is not much better than that of any other nation, since World War II we have a pretty convincing record of standing by our allies. All parties concerned are therefore convinced that we *would* defend the NATO nations against attack, which both acts as an effective deterrent to Russia aggression and tends to keep the members in the alliance. If the NATO members doubted U.S. sincerity, they might be tempted to drop out of the alliance on the theory that membership in it was more likely to irk Russia into making an attack than to deter it.

Pressure by Allies

A strong force in the maintenance of international law is pressure from friendly nations. The best modern example of this force at work is probably the 1956 Suez Canal crisis.

On July 26, 1956, President Gamal Abdel Nasser, of Egypt, nationalized the Suez Canal Company. The British and French, as principal stockholders in the company, had a large financial interest in this, but they were even more concerned by the prospect of the canal being converted from an international waterway into a bottleneck for commerce subject to the whims of Egypt's changing foreign policy. Israel was also deeply concerned at having the canal under the sole control of a hostile nation which could, and probably would, bar Israeli ships from passage.

On October 29 Israel launched an attack to take over the canal. The British and French in concert issued an ultimatum to both Israel and Egypt to cease fire and withdraw all troops from the canal area. They announced that Anglo-French troops would move in to occupy the area.

When the Soviet Union threatened to come to Egypt's defense, the situation suddenly mushroomed from a regional crisis into a possible fuse for World War III. Both the Soviet Union and the United States introduced resolutions in the U.N. Security Council for action by the United Nations to end the conflict, but neither passed because the United Kingdom and France both exercised their veto powers.

U.S. Secretary of State John Foster Dulles made the first move to break the deadlock by bringing such diplomatic pressure to bear on our British and French allies that both withdrew their vetoes. The Security Council voted to send an emergency force to occupy the canal area. The Soviet Union then brought pressure on its ally, Egypt, to allow the force to land peaceably.

On November 15, 1956, a United Nations force of six thousand troops drawn from ten different nations occupied the canal zone without firing a shot, and the crisis was over. While technically the matter was resolved by United Nations action, this action was made possible only by diplomatic pressure being brought on both sides by *friends* of the nations subjected to the pressure.

DOMESTIC PUBLIC OPINION

Domestic public opinion is a factor only in democratic nations, because in communist nations and under dictatorships criticism of government policy is not allowed. The most recent example of this force at work is the public outrage in the United States that ended the war in Indochina. Without this pressure of public opinion, the United States might still be fighting there. But public opposition reached the point where it became a mandate from the people that the administration could have ignored only at the risk of political suicide.

Public opinion in this case forced the observance of international law only if you concede that U.S. involvement in Indochina was illegal in the first place, of course, which is a moot point. But even more recently an item emerged from a Senate investigating committee revealing a violation of international law by the United States about which there could be no question. A U.S. Air Force bomber pilot testified that enemy hospitals in Cambodia were routine bombing targets for U.S. planes by specific order from above, a clear and inexcusable violation of the Geneva Conventions.

Unaccountably this disclosure brought little public reaction. Possibly this was partly because the Watergate hearings, the revelation that we had been secretly bombing Cambodia, and related scandals involving our highest national officials had left the general public so stunned by the amorality in high office that further outrage was impossible. But it was probably also partly due to the factor that the war was over at the time the pilot testified, and public indignation is never as great over injustices committed in the past, which it is too late to rectify, as it is over matters capable of being corrected.

SANCTIONS

Sanctions come closer to the enforcement procedures of municipal law than any other force of international law because they are punitive in nature. Sanctions can take any of three forms, or combinations of the three. They may be economic, political, or military. They also may be imposed either unilaterally—that is, by a single nation against another nation—or collectively by a group of allies or by an international organization.

Economic sanctions include such devices as boycotts against the goods of the offending nation, embargoes that refuse entry of the offending nation's ships to embargoed ports and prohibit the departure of ships already in port, and reprisals such as confiscating property owned by the offending nation of equivalent value to property confiscated by it. These devices may be used unilaterally or collectively. The U.N. Charter specifically authorizes the Security Council to use economic sanctions upon vote approval by the membership, subject, of course, to veto by any of the permanent members.

Unilateral political sanctions include such things as breaking off diplomatic relations. A collective political sanction might be the suspension of a nation from an international organization, with the attendant loss of the privileges of membership. An example of the latter was the 1962 suspension of Cuba from the Organization of American States because of subversive activities by Cuba in attempting to promote communist uprisings in other Latin American nations. (Cuba has since been readmitted.)

The ultimate military sanction is war, but military intervention often occurs in a degree less than a declared war. Thus, after the April, 1965, revolution in the Dominican Republic, President Lyndon Johnson sent in U.S. Marines, ostensibly to safeguard American lives, but actually to prevent a communist take-over. While this action was clearly in violation of the Organization of American States Charter, the OAS legalized it by quickly voting to form an Inter-American Peace Force, which included the American troops already in the Dominican Republic among the contingents later sent there from Brazil, Costa Rica, El Salvador, and Nicaragua.

The U.N. Security Council is also empowered to vote the use of military force in order to preserve peace. So far it has done so five times.

In June, 1950, the Security Council used this power by passing a resolution recommending member nations to "furnish such assistance to the Republic of Korea as may be necessary to repel the armed attack [by North Korea] and to restore international peace." Although the Soviet Union was opposed to such intervention in Korea, it was boycotting the Security Council at the time, and the Soviet Union representative was therefore not present to exercise his veto. Consequently the first "police action" by the United Nations, known in American history books as the Korean War, took place despite disapproval by one of the permanent members of the Security Council—a development that has resulted in no permanent member of the Council ever again boycotting it.

Other U.N. police actions were the already mentioned 1956 U.N. Emergency Force sent to occupy the Suez Canal zone, the 1960 force sent to the Congo during the civil war there, and the 1964 peace-keeping force sent to Cyprus to prevent clashes between the Greek and Turkish communities on the island, which it was feared might trigger war between Greece and Turkey. The fifth, and most recent, was the peace-keeping force sent to monitor the Arab-Israeli cease-fire in the Mideast in October, 1973.

IT'S A SMALL WORLD

The mere fact that modern communications and rapid intercontinental transportation have destroyed the once popular concept of isolationism is an inducement for international cooperation. George Washington's advice in his farewell address to "steer clear of permanent alliances with any portion of the foreign world" was given at a time when the oceans formed such impregnable bastions of defense that the United States could safely ignore events taking place in other parts of the world. In an age when huge bombers can span the oceans in only hours and guided missiles can be directed at any target in the world from launching pads anywhere else in the world, Washington's once wise words have become meaningless. All nations, even those halfway around the world from each other, have become neighbors whether they like it or not.

It is true that until recently Communist China, with nearly a fourth of the world's population, was relatively isolated from a good portion of the rest of the world. This was not by choice, however, but was largely because the Western powers, led by the United States, had deliberately isolated her. Now that China has finally entered the world community, no developed portion of the globe remains truly isolated from the rest of the world. Like the tenants of a crowded apartment house, nations *have* to cooperate, simply because they come into such frequent contact.

This does not mean that intimate and constant contact has made the world one big happy family. Actually, since World War II, three separate groups of nations with often differing interests have formed. These are the communist nations, the anticommunist nations, and the neutral nations.

Up to now the communist group has been led by the Soviet Union, but its leadership is being increasingly challenged by China. Who will eventually emerge as leader, or if leadership will eventually be divided between them, is in the realm of pure speculation.

The anticommunist nations, which consist of most of the nations of Western Europe, North America, a good part of Central and South America, and some nations with similar international attitudes, such as Australia, are led by the United States.

The neutral group consists of a mixture of undeveloped nations that have been in existence for some time and newly independent nations, which were formerly either colonial possessions or U.N. trusteeships. Because about half the nations in the world have gained independence only within the past generation, this is a sizable bloc, but it is not as influential as the other two simply because it contains no superpowers. No particular nation leads this group, and its international interests are not nearly as clearly defined as are those of the other two groups. Nor is membership in this group as sharply distinguished as in the other two. For example, many Latin American nations have to be classed as undeveloped, but their cultural heritage is closer to that of the Western powers than to that of the neutral group. In the case of Cuba the political leaning is toward the communist bloc, as was Chile's also prior to the September, 1973, military coup that ended with the death of Marxist-leaning President Salvador Allende.

Under both Nikolai Lenin and Joseph Stalin the Soviet approach to international law was the pragmatic one that all rules and applications of law were evaluated in terms of their usefulness to the cause of spreading communism throughout the world. Both leaders made it clear in numerous public statements that the underlying aim of all Soviet foreign policy was the eventual overthrow of all capitalist systems and the worldwide triumph of communism. To attain that end, both men held to the pragmatic philosophy that the end justified the means. As a result the Soviet Union gained a worldwide reputation for observing international law only when it was to its self-interest.

After the death of Stalin the term "peaceful coexistence" began to appear in the Soviet pronouncements concerning international relations. By this term the Soviet Union does not mean to imply that it has given up the aim of eventual worldwide communism, but only that it has accepted the fact that the take-over must be by peaceful means. The nuclear age has simply made armed aggression too dangerous a method of advancing the communist cause, and the Soviet Union has pragmatically settled for fighting capitalism on political and economic levels.

While it hasn't been too successful on the political

level, the only Marxist regime in the Western hemisphere ever to gain power by ballot—Chile—collapsing in chaos after three troubled years in office, it has demonstrated that it can hold its own in economic infighting with capitalism. In the previously mentioned wheat treaty of 1972 the Soviet Union slickered the United States in a manner that would have brought gasps of admiration from a Yankee horse trader. Buying more grain than it actually needed (a total of 440 million bushels of surplus wheat) at $1.63 a bushel, it is alleged to have resold the surplus to Italy for $4.65 a bushel.

The concept of peaceful coexistence seems to be a sincere one, though, and its effect has been to make the Soviet Union more reliable in its international dealings. There is still an element of the-end-justifies-the-means thinking in its foreign policy—as illustrated by the Hungarian and Czechoslovakian incidents—but for the most part the Soviet Union seems to have developed a new sensitivity to world opinion and to be practicing a policy of observing international law more carefully than ever before.

During the Cold War years following World War II the prime foreign policy aim of the Western powers and the United States was the containment of communism. The "domino theory" that if one nation in a specific area—in Southeast Asia, for instance—fell to communism, all other nations in that area would eventually fall also, was our prime motive for involvement both in Korea and in Indochina. While that theory has not been abandoned by the United States—or at least by the present administration—it is no longer held so inflexibly by most of our allies.

Although there has been a definite thaw in the relations between the communist nations and the Western powers, the basic foreign policies of both groups remain the same. The communist nations still hope for eventual worldwide communism; the United States and its allies hope to prevent communism from spreading any farther than it has. But the mutual desire to avoid nuclear warfare and to curb the economically disastrous cost of a competitive arms race has induced each side to attempt to convince the other that it can be trusted to respect agreements, with a consequential good effect on the observance of international law.

Another factor inducing respect for international law by both power blocs has been the emergence of the neutralist bloc of nations. Competition for its favor has caused both sides to try to create the impression of being law-abiding. Both the communist bloc and the anticommunist nations also want the neutralist nations to accept international law, and both groups therefore have an incentive to be good examples.

The net result is that general respect for international law is probably at a higher level right now than ever before in history.

Chapter VI

PROCEDURES FOR THE SETTLEMENT OF DISPUTES

The basic procedures by which international disputes
are settled peacefully are outlined in two multilateral
treaties: the Hague Convention for the Pacific Settlement of International Disputes, executed in 1899 and
amended in 1907, and the United Nations Charter. The
former, still in effect after nearly seventy-five years, has
62 signatories, including all major powers. The latter
has 135.

Disputes between nations may cover a vast range of
subjects, but some of the more common causes are: (1)
breach of treaty, (2) refusal of a new nation to honor
agreements made by the previous government ruling the
territory, (3) differing boundary claims, (4) conflicting
territorial claims, (5) violations of territorial waters or
airspace, (6) intervention in the internal affairs of one
nation by another, (7) failure to observe diplomatic immunity, (8) damage to the persons or property of foreign nationals, (9) confiscation of property or nationalization of industries without proper compensation, (10)
belligerent acts.

The procedures for settling disputes will be discussed
in this chapter.

NEGOTIATION

Negotiation is the commonest method of settling disputes, and the one almost always first attempted. This is
true both in municipal law and in international law. In
the United States it is estimated that in nine out of ten
civil cases a negotiated settlement is reached out of

court. Probably the percentage of international disputes settled by negotiation without going any further is even higher.

In order to facilitate the carrying on of business with other nations, each nation sends representatives to reside in the nations with which it has diplomatic relations, so that immediate and constant contact is possible with the governments of those nations. Diplomatic representatives are called ambassadors, envoys, or ministers. An ambassador is the highest diplomatic representative, but the difference between ambassadors and the lower ranks of diplomatic representatives is merely one of prestige and privilege. Envoys and ministers have the same function as ambassadors, but lower rank because they are usually accredited to smaller nations. Until 1893 the United States never accredited a foreign representative of higher rank than envoy extraordinary and minister plenipotentiary to any nation, but that year Congress raised to ambassador level all foreign ministers to nations that sent ambassadors to us.

Governments are also represented within the geographic territories of other nations by consuls, whose duties involve servicing the needs of their own nationals traveling or residing in foreign nations, and protecting the commercial interests of their own nation. As their functions are purely administrative, however, they are not diplomatic representatives.

Some nations, including the United States, also employ ambassadors-at-large. This title gives ambassador rank to a representative not accredited to any particular nation, but employed for special missions, such as the arrangement of summit conferences.

An ambassador has equal rank with the head of state to which he is accredited and may request audience with its chief executive at any time. He and his household are immune to local law and are exempt from taxes and duties. The embassy building and grounds are regarded as part of his own nation's territory, and therefore cannot be entered by police, even with a warrant.

An ambassador cannot be arrested even for murder, his immunity to local law being absolute. The only action the nation he is accredited to may take in the event of his misbehavior is to declare him *persona non grata* (an unacceptable person) and request his government to replace him with a different ambassador.

The first move in negotiating the settlement of a dispute is for the ambassador of the aggrieved nation to present a *note of protest* either to the Minister of Foreign Affairs (the Secretary of State in the case of the United States) or to the head of state of the offending nation. A classic example of how an exchange of notes can settle a dispute without the matter going any further is the Panama Canal tolls dispute between the United States and Great Britain in 1913.

In 1901 the United States and Great Britain had signed the Hay-Pauncefote Treaty (still in effect) which in part provided that the Panama Canal should be "free and open to the vessels of commerce and war of all nations observing these Rules, on terms of entire equality." In 1913 Congress passed the Panama Tolls Act, providing for refund to U.S. vessels of tolls paid for using the canal.

The ambassador from Great Britain presented a note of protest to President Woodrow Wilson which stated in part, "The mere conferring by Congress of a power to fix lower tolls on United States ships than on British ships amounts to denial of the right of British shipping to equality of treatment. . . ."

In a note of reply the United States held that the term "all nations" did not include the United States, since she had built and owned the canal, and certainly had not intended when she signed the Hay-Pauncefote Treaty to give up the right of preferential treatment for her own ships, especially since the treatment did not alter the tolls paid by other nations' ships.

Another note from the British ambassador declared that the terms of the treaty were "definite and explicit" and that "all nations" did include the United States.

Great Britain's protest was not in the expectation of having its ships' tolls refunded also, an obvious impossibility since all other nations would then be entitled to similar treatment, leaving the United States in the position of operating a toll-free canal. The bone of contention was that the preferential treatment given to U.S. shipping gave it an unfair competitive advantage over other nations in contracting for cargoes. Because the overhead of canal tolls was eliminated, U.S. ships would be able to take business away from British ships.

Senator Elihu Root, former Secretary of War, former Secretary of State, and one of the most powerful members of the Senate, sided with Great Britain and managed to convert President Wilson to his point of view. On March 5, 1914, the President appeared before a joint session of Congress to ask repeal of the Panama Tolls Act. His plea, "We are too self-respecting a nation to interpret with too strained or refined reading the words of our own promises, just because we have power enough to give us leave to read them as we please," stirred the Congress to repeal the act.

Thus a major controversy between the United States and Great Britain was averted by nothing more elaborate than an exchange of diplomatic notes.

GOOD OFFICES

Article 3 of the Hague Convention provides that "powers stranger to the dispute have the right to offer good offices or mediation even during the course of hostilities. . . . The exercise of this right can never be regarded by either of the parties in dispute as an unfriendly act."

Good offices are offered, usually, only after diplomatic relations have been broken between the disputing nations. It is a matter of customary law that the nation offering its good offices must not have a selfish interest in the dispute. It is supposed to be an act of friendship to both parties, neither for the benefit of either disputant nor to the benefit of the nation offering the service. Nations are usually very careful to make sure that the Hague Convention provision prohibiting either disputant from regarding the offer of good offices as an unfriendly act is justified.

The offer of good offices is merely an offer to act as a go-between in an effort to get the disputing parites to resume negotiations and thus avoid war. It is not an offer to mediate the dispute, but only to arrange for resumption of contact (although sometimes the disputants ask the good-offices nation to act as a mediator after they resume contact). Either party has the right to reject good offices.

If the offer is accepted by both parties, or all parties if it is a multilateral dispute, the nation providing good offices then meets separately—never jointly—with representatives of the disputing parties to work out terms for resuming negotiations. Once contacts between the disputants is resumed, the role of the good-offices nation is over.

Offers of good offices may come not only from third-party nations but from the International Committee of the Red Cross, the Secretary-General of the United Nations, or the Security Council. For instance, in 1947 the Security Council, with the consent of both parties, appointed a Good Offices Committee consisting of Australia, Belgium, and the United States to bring about negotiations between the emerging Indonesian Republic and the Netherlands, of which Indonesia had formerly been a possession, concerning the details of the new nation's independence.

Prior to entering both World War I and World War II the United States offered its good offices to the belligerents, but there were no takers in either case. Switzerland more successfully used good offices to end hostilities between the United States and Japan at the end of World War II, transmitting the offers and counter-offers of both nations to each other until the armistice terms were finally agreed upon.

MEDIATION

Mediation goes further than the use of good offices in that the mediator actively participates in the settlement of the dispute. Mediation may be undertaken by a neutral nation, by a group of nations, by an international organization, or by an individual or group of individuals.

The mediator must be acceptable to both disputants. Regardless of which type of the various possible types of mediator he is, he is expected to offer suggestions for the settlement of the dispute instead of merely presiding over negotiations. His suggestions are always in the category of advice, though, and under no circumstances are ever binding on either party. However, he does work directly with both parties, sometimes meeting with them separately, sometimes jointly. His mission is complete either when the dispute is settled or when a hopeless impasse is reached.

One of the most famous cases of mediation in the United States was by President Theodore Roosevelt at the end of the Russo-Japanese War in 1905. Japan had won decisive naval victories in the Pacific and also a decisive land victory in Korea. In order to continue the war, Japan was going to have to press her attack across Siberia to European Russia. She had no stomach for that, and Czarist Russia, crippled by strikes and mutinies in opposition to the war, devoutly wanted an end to hostilities also. The situation had reached a stage where further fighting was pointless, but it continued because neither side wanted to admit weakness by suggesting peace.

When President Roosevelt offered to mediate, both jumped at the opportunity to quit fighting without losing face. A conference of Russian, Japanese, and United States representatives met at Portsmouth, New Hampshire, on August 5, 1905, and ended in a peace treaty a month later. Under the treaty's terms Russia acknowledged Japan's preeminence in Korea, ceded half of Sakhalin Island to Japan, and made some other concessions. Both parties jointly agreed to evacuate Manchuria and restore it to China. Japan demanded an indemnity, which Russia declined to pay, but eventually dropped that claim.

While the terms as a whole were more favorable to Japan than to Russia, this was the era of power politics, when it was generally accepted that the victor in warfare deserved some rewards of victory. As Japan was definitely the "winner" of the Russo-Japanese War, the settlement was regarded in the international community as eminently just.

COMMISSIONS OF INQUIRY

The Hague Convention provided for the maintenance of a permanent list of commissioners to conduct inquiries into the facts of international disputes, from which five were to be selected for each specific inquiry. Each party to a dispute was entitled to choose two commissioners, only one of which could be a name it had personally submitted to the list. The fifth commissioner was to be chosen by the other four.

Commissions of inquiry are limited to investigations and reports as to facts, and make no recommendations as to settlements or awards. The most famous example of inquiry under the Hague Convention was the Dogger Bank Case of 1904.

During the Russo-Japanese War Admiral Zinovi Petrovich Rozhdestvensky, of the Russian Navy, mistook some fog-shrouded British fishing trawlers of the Dogger Bank in the North Sea for Japanese torpedo boats and ordered them fired upon. One trawler was sunk, another damaged, and two fishermen were killed. Great Britain demanded an apology, damages, and punishment of the admiral.

At the suggestion of the French Government, Great Britain and Russia both agreed to the appointment of a commission of inquiry. The commission chosen consisted of five admirals, one each from the British, Russian, French, Austrian, and United States navies. After investigation the commission reported that the firing had no justification, but that it had been a mistake attributable to low visibility rather than a deliberately hostile act and that the circumstances cast no reflection upon either the military efficiency or humanitarianism of Admiral Rozhdestvensky and his men.

This report is particularly instructive concerning an

extremely important factor in the settlement of international disputes, whether the method used is mediation, conciliation, arbitration, or adjudication. That factor is the necessity to save face for all parties. The clearing of Russia of any deliberate fault, yet the fixing of responsibility on her for damages, saved her humiliation in the eyes of the world and thus made her much more amenable to negotiating the payment of damages to Great Britain. The amount eventually paid was £65,000 for property damage and to indemnify the families of the two dead fishermen.

Only two other commissions of inquiry were appointed under the Hague Convention prior to the formation of the League of Nations, when that body took over the appointment of such commissions. Six commissions operated under League sponsorship, the last being the commission to investigate the Manchurian crisis of 1931.

On September 18, 1931, a bomb exploded on the track of the Japanese-run South Manchurian Railroad near Mukden. Japan, long seeking an excuse to invade Manchuria, seized on the incident to justify its military occupation of southern Manchuria. Chiang Kai-shek, then China's leader, protested to the League of Nations.

The commission of inquiry appointed by the League found that "an explosion undoubtedly occurred on or near the railroad between 10:00 and 10:30 A.M. on September 18th, but the damage, if any, to the railroad did not in fact prevent the punctual arrival of the southbound train from Changchun, and was not in itself sufficient to justify military action. The military action of the Japanese . . . cannot be regarded as measures of legitimate self-defense."

On the basis of this report the League Council condemned the invasion and requested the withdrawal of Japanese troops from Manchuria. As a face-saving device for Japan, the League also requested China to withdraw its forces from there. Although technically under the command of Chiang Kai-shek, these were really Manchurian troops, so that actually the League was requesting an invaded nation to get its own troops out of the country.

Japan informed the League that she had no territorial designs on Manchuria, and on September 30 both Japan and China agreed to withdraw their forces.

Up to that point the whole incident was an example of the effectiveness of commission of inquiry, but then occurred one of the things that make the workings of international law so unpredictable. Chang Hsueh-liang, the warload ruler of Manchuria known as the Young Marshal, withdrew his troops below the Great Wall into China proper in conformity with China's agreement. And Japan promptly took over the rest of Manchuria.

Since World War II, commissions of inquiry have fallen into disuse, largely because the machinery of the United Nations has made them unnecessary. Since the Security Council is empowered to investigate any situation that threatens the peace, outside commissions of inquiry are superfluous. The machinery is still available to disputing nations, though, if at any time they desire to use it.

CONCILIATION

Conciliation is a combination of inquiry and mediation. The conciliation commission, council, committee, or whatever it happens to be called not only investigates the circumstances of a dispute but recommends a settlement. It is a less flexible procedure than mediation in that a mediator may continue to make one suggestion after another until he finally hits on one acceptable to all parties, whereas a conciliation group usually submits only a single report at the end of the inquiry, outlining the facts as they have been found to be and recommending a settlement. The parties are not bound by the report but are free either to accept or to reject it.

In actual practice the process is not so greatly different from mediation as it may seem at first glance. While there is only a single report and recommendation made, the report is always preceded by thorough consultation with all parties to the dispute, so that the conciliators are aware of what will be acceptable to the disputants. The recommended settlement therefore often stems from a process quite similar to mediation.

While the process of arriving at a recommendation for settlement is similar to mediation, conciliation as a device differs in three ways:

1. It is normally carried on by a commission or committee appointed by a group or organization such as the United Nations or one of the regional organizations described in Chapter IV, rather than by a single nation or individual, as in mediation. Quite often treaties include a clause providing for conciliation by a specific organization, such as the Organization of American States or the Organization of African Unity, in the event of dispute.

2. Its proposals usually carry more weight than those of a mediator, even though they are no more binding. This is because the commission usually represents an important bloc of powers. In example, let us assume that in two disputes between Peru and Bolivia, one is mediated by mutual agreement by Colombia, and the other is referred to the OAS for conciliation. The conciliation commission appointed by the OAS consists of representatives of Nicaragua, Argentina, Brazil, Mexico, and the United States. Obviously the combined influence of the last five nations is going to carry considerably more weight than the single nation of Colombia.

3. It is a more formal proceeding than mediation, usually involving the holding of scheduled sessions and the hearing of witnesses, much like a Senate investigating committee such as Senator Sam Ervin's so-called Watergate Committee.

Although there is no rule of customary law concerning it, conciliation commissions usually consist of five members.

Disputes settled by conciliation in the years since World War II include a 1947 boundary dispute between France and Thailand, a 1949 dispute between Romania and Switzerland, a 1952 Danish-Belgian dispute, two disputes in 1955 between France and Switzerland, and one in 1956 between Greece and Italy. None of these had particularly interesting facets, however. For one of the most interesting conciliation cases, and also one of the most illustrative as to how conciliation works, we have to go back to 1927.

The Versailles Treaty at the end of World War I placed the coal-rich Saar Basin Territory of Germany under the administration of the League of Nations. As reparation for the destruction of French coal mines by the German Army, France was granted exclusive production rights to the Saar Basin coal mines for a period of fifteen years. In order to protect this operation, France kept a police force of eight hundred men in the area. Ostensibly this was a League of Nations force, but everyone knew it was all French and was employed solely to protect French interests, not those of the League.

By 1927 the presence of French police on what the German people considered German soil, despite the area being technically a League-administered territory, had become not only a matter of friction between the French and German governments but a stormy public issue. German newspapers began to demand editorially that the "disguised military occupation" end. French newspapers hotly rejoined that the unruly population of the Saar Basin required a large police force.

Public opinion became so strong in both nations that it pressured both governments into deadlocked positions from which neither could afford to retreat. In Germany public sentiment demanded that if the "League" police force was not withdrawn, or at least substantially reduced, Germany should withdraw from the League. Having joined only the year before, the German Government had no desire to do that, but as it was an elected government, it would hardly be politically expedient to ignore public opinion on so hot an issue. In France public opposition to the withdrawal of even a single policeman was so great that the government was in danger of falling if it made a concession.

The situation was one in which the peoples of both nations were angrier at each other than were their governments. Both governments hoped for a solution, and in that mood for compromise asked for conciliation by the League of Nations. Because of the seriousness of the situation, the League Council, instead of appointing a commission, decided to act as the conciliation agent itself. Hearings were therefore held before the entire council.

As the hearings proceeded, both sides maintained a public attitude of no compromise, but behind the scenes the conciliators discovered that Germany would accept the compromise of France withdrawing three hundred men and leaving a force of five hundred. Unfortunately the French delegates, while willing to compromise in some other way, if such a way could be found, were unwilling to agree to the withdrawal of any men at all.

The stalemate was finally ended by an ingenious suggestion made by the Italian delegate to the League Council. He suggested that France keep its forces of eight hundred police, but place three hundred of them in reserve, so that never more than five hundred would be visible to the public at any one time.

When the concilation report recommended this Solomon-like solution, it was accepted with relief by both sides, again illustrating the importance in international relations of saving face, or preserving the prestige of all parties concerned.

ARBITRATION

The main difference between arbitration and the previous methods of settlement studied is that arbtiration results in a *decision* instead of merely a recommendation. And that decision is binding.

Arbitration, like all other devices for the settlement of international disputes, is submitted to only by mutual consent of the parties concerned. Usually the consent is expressed in the form of a treaty specifying who the arbitrator is to be, or the composition of the arbitral tribunal if more than one person is to arbitrate, specifically defining the dispute to be arbitrated and, sometimes, specifying certain rules or principles of law that must be followed by the arbitrators. This last item is best explained by giving an example.

During the Civil War British shipbuilders built and sold to the Confederate states several warships. Following the war, the United States claimed damages from Great Britain for the shipping sunk by these vessels. For purposes of simplification the claims were all lumped together under the name of one of the ships, called the *Alabama*, to become known as the Alabama Claims.

A treaty signed at Washington in May, 1871, provided for arbitration of the claim by a five-man commission consisting of representatives of the United States, Great Britain, Italy, Switzerland, and Brazil. At United States insistence the treaty laid down two rules that were to govern the arbitrators in arriving at their decision. The first was that a neutral government was bound to "use due diligence" to prevent the fitting out, arming, and equipping within its jurisdiction of any vessel that it had reasonable grounds to believe was intended to be used as a warship against any nation with which it was at peace. The second was that it could not permit either belligerent to use its ports.

While Great Britain refused to accept these rules as principles of international law in force at the time the claims arose, since that would have been an admission that she had deliberately broken international law, she agreed to accept them as rules to be applied in this particular case and in future similar cases. The stipulation in effect admitted responsibility, but not guilt. It was an expensive admission, because the commission awarded the United States damages in the amount of $15.5 million.

Although a single person may be appointed to act as an arbitrator, most arbitration treaties provide for a three-man commission, one selected by each side and the third chosen by the other two. A majority vote rather than a unaminous vote is usually all that is required for a decision. Usually the choices of the disputants are from their own nations, but it is accepted customary law that they are not to consider themselves representatives of their own countries, but as impartial dispensers of justice. The third choice is invariably from a neutral country.

The Hague Convention provided for a Permanent Court of Arbitration, but actually it was neither permanent nor a court. It was merely a list of names similar to the list maintained for commissions of inquiry. Each nation signatory to the treaty supplied four names. When a dispute arose, each party selected an equal number of names from the list (usually either one or two), and those selected chose one more from the list to act as umpire.

The Permanent Court of Arbitration has been used infrequently. Between 1899 and 1932 it handed down only twenty decisions. Although still legally in existence, because the Hague Convention is still in force, since 1932 it has heard only three cases. The main reason for this seems to be that from the beginning it was regarded as a court rather than as a mechanism for arbitration, and therefore nations continued to select arbitrators from other sources, submitting to the Permanent Court of Arbitration only matters normally considered appropriate for adjudication. Probably the reason it has now fallen into virtual disuse is that the League of Nation's Permanent Court of International Justice, and later the U.N.'s International Court of Justice, got the type of cases formerly submitted to the Permanent Court of Arbitration.

A unique arbitral decision, cited only for its interest and not as a representative case, as it has neither precedent nor subsequent example, was the Aaroo Mountain dispute of 1932. Aaroo Mountain is on the border between Yemen and Saudi Arabia. When Yemen troops occupied the mountain, Saudi Arabia protested that it was an invasion of its territory. Yemen replied that the mountain was within the territorial limits of Yemen, and that besides, the inhabitants of the mountain had requested military protection. When negotiations over who owned the mountain finally broke down, the Imam of Yemen impulsively sent a telegram to King Ibn Saud, of Saudi Arabia, asking that he arbitrate the matter. The

Imam agreed to abide by whatever decision Ibn Saud gave.

Ibn Saud consented to act as arbitrator and decided against himself.

ADJUDICATION

The only difference between adjudication and arbitration is that adjudication is before a formal and permanent judical body, whereas arbitration is before a temporary commission or committee chosen to decide a specific case. Decisions by either body are equally binding.

While the device of arbitration goes clear back into the dim reaches of history, the concept of an international court to settle international disputes by adjudication is a relatively new one. As has already been mentioned, the Hague Convention's Permanent Court of Arbitration was not actually a court. The first real international court, in the sense of being a permanent judicial body with jurisdiction over international disputes, was only a regional one. The Central American Court of Justice was created in 1907 by a miltilateral treaty signed by five Central American nations. The court consisted of five judges and was located in Cartago, Costa Rica. It was empowered to hear cases between nations party to the treaty, cases between any nation party to the treaty and an outside nation, and claims by nationals of any of the five nations against one of the other signatory nations. In all cases its jurisdiction was dependent upon agreement by all parties concerned that the court should hear the case.

In 1917 the court was mortally wounded when it handed down a judgment in favor of El Salvador and Costa Rica against Nicaragua, and Nicaragua refused to accept the decision. When it was unable to enforce its decision, the other four nations lost confidence in it, and it quietly expired.

In 1923 the same five Central American nations signed another treaty creating an International Central-American Tribunal similar to the original court, but the administrative work of actually establishing the court was never completed, so it never came into existence.

These were the only two efforts to create a permanent international judicial body prior to the Permanent Court of International Justice under the League of Nations, and that was the first international court with worldwide jurisdiction. As has been mentioned, the present Court is regarded as a continuation of that Court, rather than as an entirely new one. The Statute of the present Court, for instance, keeps "alive" clauses in treaties still in force that called for referral of disputes to the Permanent Court of International Justice, so that the present Court can deal with them if disputes arise.

Since the International Court of Justice was thoroughly covered in Chapter II, its organization and functions will not be repeated here. However, a few more comments about it are in order.

The Court handles two distinct types of proceedings: disputes between nations, which require it to render judgments, and advisory proceedings in which it merely gives legal opinions. It has hardly been deluged with either type of case, though. In the criminal courts of the city of Manhattan alone there are between three hundred and four hundred indictments *daily*. In contrast the International Court of Justice during its entire existence has rendered twelve advisory opinions, its predecessor handed down something like forty decisions in disputes between nations, and the present Court during its nearly thirty years of existence has handled fewer than thirty-five disputes.

Both its advisory opinions and its judgments have had profound influence on the development of international law, though. Some of its more important advisory opinions have concerned such matters as the functions of the International Labor Organization, the rights of minorities, and the international status of the United Nations. In the area of international dispute, several cases stand out. The Anglo-Norwegian Fisheries Case, described in Chapter II, clarified the law on fisheries and territorial waters; the Corfu Channel Case, cited in Chapter III, established new responsibilities for nations to other nations; a 1961 dispute between Cambodia and Thailand known as the Temple of Preah Vihear Case brought an important ruling relating to title to territory.

Probably the main reason that the International Court of Justice is used so sparingly is that it is a last resort, after all other methods of settlement have failed. But there is also a tendency even in last-resort situations to use smaller or more specialized tribunals, when these are available. International claims that could be referred to the ICJ are often brought in municipal courts instead. Two such instances, a case before the U.S. Supreme Court and another before the Civil Tribunal of Venice, have been cited in this book. More often regional tribunals or arbitration commissions are chosen in lieu of the ICJ, however.

The International Court of Justice is far from dead, though. And its mere availability tends to act as a deterrent to the breaking of international law.

As this is written, three cases are before the Court. Technically there are five, but in two instances two separate cases involve the same set of circumstances, and although there are two plaintiff nations in each instance, the ICJ is hearing each pair of cases together.

The *Trial of Pakistani Prisoners of War Case* (Pakistan versus India) stems from India's announcement that she intends to try 195 Pakistani prisoners of war and civilian internees for genocide. Pakistan denied India's right to try the prisoners and requested an interim injunction against the trial until the Court could hear the evidence. As a result of negotiations between the two nations, this request was later withdrawn, but the case itself remains on the Court's list. As of the winter of 1973 hearings were still being held.

The *Fisheries Jurisdiction Cases* (the United Kingdom versus Iceland and the Federal Republic of Germany versus Iceland) stemmed from Iceland's 1972 expansion of its territorial waters from twelve miles out to sea to fifty miles. The details of the dispute are outlined in the next chapter.

The *Nuclear Test Cases* (Australia versus France and

New Zealand versus France) began over the announcement by France in May, 1973, of its intention to conduct nuclear tests over Mururoa Atoll in the South Pacific. Australia and New Zealand simultaneously but
separately instituted proceedings against France before
the ICJ on May 9, 1973, claiming that the tests would
result in radioactive fallout on their territories, which
would violate their rights under international law. Each
asked the Court to "indicate interim measures of protection," international-law jargon meaning they wanted the
Court to issue an injunction banning the tests until the
Court had time to hear all the evidence.

On May 16 France stated that it considered the Court
"manifestly not competent in the cases" and that it
could not accept the Court's jurisdiction. Ordinarily this
would have ended the matter insofar as the ICJ was
concerned, since mutual consent to have a dispute adjudicated is a basic requirement of the Court. But world
opinion was so solidly against the proposed tests and so
much in favor of the matter being adjudicated by the
ICJ that the Court found a technicality that allowed it to
retain the cases on its list. It set hearings to decide
whether or not it had jurisdiction to hear the cases.

On the premise that it *did* have jurisdiction at least to
hear pleas concerning its own competence to decide the
case, on June 22 it issued two almost identical communiqués, one directed to Australia and France, the
other to New Zealand and France. In essence the
communiqués said that all three governments should ensure that no action of any kind was taken that might ag-
gravate the dispute, and in particular the French government should avoid nuclear tests causing the deposit of
radioactive fallout on the territories of the plaintiff nations.

Ignoring the communiqués, on July 21 France deto-
nated a nuclear device suspended from a balloon 2,000
feet over Mururoa Atoll. There was worldwide protest
over what the news media generally described as the deliberate defying of an "interim injunction" by the ICJ.
This was hardly an accurate description of the Court's
communiqués, however. Neither had the force of an in-

junction by a municipal court, which is an enforceable order. The communiqués, for all practical purposes, were merely unenforceable requests. Furthermore France had formally refused to accept the Court's jurisdiction, and the Court itself at that point had only declared its competence to hear arguments as to whether or not it had jurisdiction. The morality of the issue aside, the defiance of the communiqués per se does not appear to be a violation of international law on the part of France. She may eventually be found guilty of such violation because of damage done to the plaintiff nations by radioactive fallout, but that is quite a different matter.

On July 29 France exploded a second nuclear device at the same location. Although this registered on the detection instruments of other nations as much smaller than the first, worldwide protest was even larger. Further testing was suspended, but whether this was because of the protest or merely because the first phase of the tests was finished is unknown. No official reason for the suspension was given by the French government.

The jurisdictional question still pends before the Court. A court order dated August 28, 1973, gave the plaintiffs until November 23, 1973, to file their pleas on that question only and gave France until April, 1974, to file its counterplea. Since hearings on the basic issue of the legality of the nuclear tests cannot even begin until the jurisdictional matter is settled, no decision on that can be expected for some time.

WAR

The final method of settling international disputes when all else has failed is war. The United Nations Charter outlaws war except in the case of self-defense, and most of the world is now signatory to that Charter. Nevertheless, wars keep occurring, and each one has to be a violation of international law by at least one belligerent, for it is impossible for both sides to be fighting in self-defense.

Often both sides *claim* to be fighting only in self-defense. As a random example, Israel's 1956 attack on the Suez Canal zone was claimed to be self-defense because Egypt's closing of the canal would destroy Israel economically. Egypt was also able to claim self-defense, because there was no question that she was under attack.

In the 1973 war Egypt and Syria appeared to make the initial attack on Israel, but again both sides claimed the other attacked first.

Since World War II there have been literally hundreds of armed conflicts throughout the world, though many of them were not officially designated as wars—both Korea and Vietnam, for instance. These, so far, have all been "contained" wars involving no direct clash between any of the superpowers, although military personnel of superpowers have sometimes opposed each other in combat in the role of "advisers."

A direct military clash between any of the superpowers, with its attendant risk of nuclear war, seems less and less likely as time goes on, particularly during the present era of thawed relations. It is by no means an impossibility, however, and remains a potential horror we have to live with as the main penalty of our advanced technology.

Chapter VII

THE LAW OF THE SEA

In 1958 four conventions were signed at Geneva codifying the law of the sea. The United States is signatory to only three of them: the Convention on the High Seas, which to date has been ratified or acceded to by fifty-one nations; the Convention on the Continental Shelf, also with fifty-one nations party to it; the Convention on the Territorial Sea and Contiguous Zone, with forty-two nations so far party to it. The United States has not ratified the Convention on Fishing and Conservation of the Living Resources of the High Seas.

In 1968 the U.N. General Assembly appointed an eighty-six-member Committee on the Peaceful Uses of the Sea-Bed and the Ocean Floor Beyond the Limits of National Jurisdiction (since expanded to ninety-one members) which resulted in scheduling a Conference on the Law of the Sea to be held at Santiago, Chile, in 1974. The convention expected to come from that conference, which will have to do with the protection and conservation of mineral resources in the seabed and the prevention of pollution, will probably bear the same title as the committee.

In 1971 a multilateral treaty was simultaneously signed at Washington, D.C., London, and Moscow bearing the lengthy title *Treaty on the Prohibition of the Emplacement of Nuclear Weapons and Other Weapons of Mass Destruction on the Seabed and the Ocean Floor and in the Subsoil Thereof*. This treaty, which has forty-five signatories and went into effect for the United States on May 18, 1972, is sometimes cited as an additional codification of the law of the sea, because it tends to encourage the peaceful use of the seabed and ocean floor. However, since the sole motive behind it was arms control, it is probably more properly classified in that category than as a part of the law of the sea.

The four present conventions and the one expected to be drafted at Santiago, Chile, pretty thoroughly codify the law of the sea in all areas except fishing. (So many nations signatory to the Convention on Fishing and Conservation of the Living Resources of the High Seas ratified or acceded to it with reservations, or with understanding and interpretation concerning the fisheries clauses, that fishing rules can in no sense be considered to have general international acceptance.) Although these conventions are legally binding only on the nations signatory to them, their wide acceptance probably puts them in the category of customary law, which means that even nations not party to them will be expected to abide by the rules they lay down.

What is referred to as "the sea" under international law is divided into three zones: internal waters, territorial waters, and the high seas.

INTERNAL WATERS

Internal waters consist of ports, harbors, rivers, lakes, and canals. Such waters may be used by foreign vessels only with the permission of the coastal nation, but customarily general permission to use its internal waters under specified rules is granted by treaty to the nations with which the coastal nation customarily engages in trade. Under customary law ships in distress are excepted from the rule requiring permission and are also exempt from harbor duties or other taxes normally imposed by the coastal nation.

As most nations have no desire to restrict trade, disputes concerning the right of entry into internal waters are so rare that the subject is hardly important enough to discuss. What is important, and what has created some dispute, is the legal status of foreign ships after entering internal waters. That status depends on whether the ship is a merchant vessel or a warship.

Under customary law foreign merchant ships in internal waters are subject to the municipal law of coastal nations. Thus, in the 1923 U.S. Supreme Court ruling in *Cunard v. Mellon,* employees of the Cunard line were held guilty of serving liquor to passengers within American internal waters in violation of the Eighteenth Amendment, even though this was legal in the ship's own nation.

There are some exceptions to this rule of customary law. One is that the coastal nation's jurisdiction is not exclusive. A crime committed aboard a merchant ship may also be tried by the nation whose flag the ship flies, and usually is if the crime does not affect the interest of the coastal nation or any of its nationals. The general rule is that if there has been no disturbance of the coastal nation's peace or security, the flag nation has jurisdiction over crimes committed aboard ship. Another exception is that the coastal nation cannot interfere with the discipline of a captain over his crew, even if it involves acts illegal in the coastal nation (e.g., flogging).

The rules governing the peaceful presence of warships in internal waters are quite different. They, and their crew members, are immune to municipal law except for navigational and health rules. Like an embassy, a warship is considered part of the territory of its nation, and coastal-nation authorities cannot even come aboard it without permission. This immunity even extends to crew members ashore in cases where they are in uniform and on official business.

There are gray areas in the distinction between merchant ship and warships where customary law is not clearly defined. This has led to some international disputes. As the merchant ships of communist nations are owned by the government rather than by private persons or companies, communist nations have claimed the same immunity for them as for warships. The Western powers are at a disadvantage in contesting such claims, because they too have some government-owned ships other than warships for which they sometimes claim immunity. The United States, for instance, has long claimed immunity for government-owned ships engaged in gathering weather data or in other scientific investigation.

TERRITORIAL WATERS

The distance out to sea from shore over which nations had jurisdiction did not become a matter of controversy until modern international law began to develop in the sixteenth century. Prior to that the ships of foreign nations did not pass near to coastal nations often enough to make the issue important. But as maritime trade increased, coastal nations began to realize the importance of maintaining control over the waters immediately off their shores.

The initial reaction was to make extravagant claims to large areas of the sea, but as these were never generally accepted by other nations, the claims gradually reduced in size. During the eighteenth century the canon-shot rule gained wide acceptance. This set the territorial limit at the range of a cannon shot, which then was approximately three miles. During the Napoleonic Wars, as cannon began to gain in range, the three-mile limit became recognized as customary law in Europe.

Later in the nineteenth century the three-mile rule gained worldwide acceptance, except in two areas. The Scandinavian nations claimed four miles, and Spain and Portugal claimed six.

During the twentieth century claims have varied so greatly that it can no longer be said that there is any rule of customary law concerning territorial limits. Only twenty-one nations of the eighty-six attending the Geneva Conference on the Law of the Sea in 1958 were willing to accept the territorial three-mile limit, although all the major maritime powers accepted it. Nineteen claimed between five and ten miles offshore, thirty claimed twelve miles, and six claimed in excess of twelve miles.

The main factor responsible for destroying the customary rule of a three-mile limit has been fishing rights. The relatively shallow areas of the ocean near to shore are the best for commercial fishing. Prior to the twentieth century there was little conflict of interest over fishing rights because it was economically feasible to fish only areas close to the fishermen's home ports. Because fishing trawlers lacked refrigeration, the catch would spoil if it had to be brought from a long distance. Peruvian fishermen might fish off the coast of Chile, but no Russian, British, Japanese, or even United States fishing trawlers would be found there. Furthermore, fishing techniques were still primitive enough so that there was little danger of fishing beds being depleted, and consequently coastal nations had no great objection to the trawlers of nearby nations fishing off their coasts.

That has all changed drastically. Modern trawlers are equipped with refrigeration, making it possible for them to roam thousands of miles from their home ports. Highly industrialized nations such as Japan, Great Britain, and the United States have developed massive floating factories that suck in everything but the smallest plankton from the sea, freeze the catch, and therefore can stay out for months at a time.

Poor nations economically dependent on the catch from their coastal waters have attempted to protect their traditional fishing beds from these monstrous vacuum cleaners by progressively moving their territorial limits farther and farther out to sea. That is what is behind the disputes mentioned in the preceding chapter between Iceland and Great Britain and Iceland and the Federal Republic of Germany.

The specifics of the disputes, which really go back twenty years, are these:

In the early 1950s Iceland increased its territorial limit from three to four miles. On the grounds that this interfered with traditional British fishing rights, Great Britain imposed economic sanctions. But the spectacle of one of the world's industrial giants economically bullying such a powerless little nation so turned world opinion against Great Britain that she had to back down. Pretty much the same thing happened when Iceland increased its territorial limit to twelve miles in 1958.

In September, 1972, Iceland unilaterally extended its limit to fifty miles and declared the area within that limit out of bounds to foreign trawlers. Since about 20 percent of the catch of the British and West German fishing industries came from those waters, both nations quite naturally protested.

At first glance these progressive extensions of territorial limits by little Iceland may seem capricious and arrogant. But when you consider that its seabeds are Iceland's sole natural resource, and that 80 percent of its exports consist of fish, it can be seen that considerable is at stake. If the seabeds are destroyed, Iceland will be destroyed. It is as simple as that.

Quite obviously new rules concerning territorial limits are necessary which take into consideration the protection of coastal nations' fishing beds. The Geneva Conference of 1958 attempted to grapple with the problem, but left it up in the air because of lack of agreement. Until it is solved, small nations can be expected to take unilateral defensive measures by pushing their territorial limits farther and farther out to sea.

For years the United States has been having disputes with the Pacific Coast nations of South America similar to the disputes of Great Britain and West Germany with Iceland. Argentina, Chile, Ecuador, and Peru have seized U.S. fishing vessels off their coasts, in some cases nearly two hundred miles offshore.

The defense of this practice has not been based on territorial limit, however, but on the 1958 Geneva Convention on Fishing and Conservation of the Living Resources of the High Seas (to which the United States is not party). As its title implies, the convention is concerned with conservation as well as with fishing, and it made an attempt to deal with the problem of conserving existing seabeds for future generations. One of the provisions was that under certain circumstances coastal nations could impose conservation rules for the waters off their coasts, subject to appeal to an international commission of experts. The South American nations have claimed that this entitles them to impose conservation measures on areas up to two hundred miles from their shores. In practice these measures consist primarily of barring foreign fishing trawlers. The larger industrial nations have not accepted this claim, and it has become a periodic source of dispute between them and the four South American nations making it.

A *contiguous zone* is an area of the high seas adjacent to territorial waters over which the coastal nation claims jurisdiction for some specific reason, such as its being a common rendezvous area for smugglers.

The right to declare jurisdiction over a contiguous zone was codified in the 1958 Convention on the Territorial Sea and the Contiguous Zone by restricting such areas to twelve miles from shore and specifying that they may be claimed only for purposes of preventing infringement of the coastal nation's "customs, fiscal, immigration or sanitary regulations."

THE HIGH SEAS

All ocean areas not part of either internal waters or territorial waters are the high seas and may be used freely by the ships of all nations. The 1958 Convention on the High Seas says that freedom of the high seas includes freedom of navigation, freedom of fishing, freedom to lay submarine cables and pipelines, and freedom to use the airspace above them.

A vessel on the high seas is subject to both international law and the laws of its flag state. Insofar as the latter is concerned, the nationality of a warship is unchanging, but this is not necessarily true of a merchant vessel. The flag a merchant vessel flies is determined by where it is registered, and quite often this is not the nation of the owner. "Flags of convenience" are more the rule than the exception in merchant shipping.

The reason for this is primarily economic. Each nation sets its own standards for merchant vessels operating under its registry. The larger maritime powers, such as the United States and the United Kingdom, have strict regulations concerning the nationality of the owners of its registered ships, the nationalities of the crews, and where the ships were built. Other nations will register virtually any ship in return for the registration fee. An odd result of this is that, on paper, the nation owning the largest tonnage of ships in the world is Liberia.

The popularity of flags of convenience stems from ships having to meet the wage and safety standards only of the nation of registry. They therefore avoid having to pay union wages and install expensive safety equipment if they are registered in such nations as Liberia or Panama instead of in the United States or Great Britain.

United States policy permits American owners to register their ships wherever they choose so long as they make them available for requisition in the event of war.

A ship must be registered somewhere, or it becomes a stateless ship, which is illegal under international law and makes it subject to seizure by any nation. But it cannot be registered in more than one nation. The Convention on the High Seas provides that if a ship sails under two or more flags, it loses the protection of all and becomes a stateless ship.

On the high seas both warships and merchant ships are considered part of the territory of the flag state and, except in time of war and under certain special peacetime circumstances, are immune to interference by the ships of other nations. The municipal law of the flag-state applies in cases of crimes committed aboard on the high seas, except in the case of piracy.

There are no circumstances under which the merchant vessel of one nation is entitled to interfere with the merchant vessel of another on the high seas without permission, but there are special circumstances under which a warship of one nation may interfere with the merchant vessel of another. These are:

1. When the merchant vessel is in a contiguous zone or an exclusive fisheries zone, it may be boarded for investigation.

2. When a merchant vessel is stateless, it may be seized. It was under this rule that the flagless ship *Asya* was arrested on the high seas in 1948 by the British navy while it was sailing illegal immigrants to Palestine, shortly before Great Britain gave up the Palestine mandate.

3. A merchant vessel may be overtaken and boarded after *hot pursuit* when fleeing from arrest or investiga-

tion from internal waters, territorial waters, or a contiguous zone. Article 23 of the Convention on the High Seas provides: "The hot pursuit of a foreign ship may be undertaken when the competent authorities of the coastal state have good reason to believe that the ship has violated the laws and regulations of that state. Such pursuit must be commenced when the foreign ship or one of its boats is within the internal waters or the territorial sea or the contiguous zone of the pursuing state, and may only be continued outside the territorial sea or the contiguous zone if the pursuit has not been interrupted." It further stipulates that pursuit may commence only after a "visual or auditory" signal to stop has been given at a distance that enables it to be seen or heard by the foreign ship, and must stop as soon as the pursued ship enters the territorial waters of its own nation or a third nation.

4. A warship has the *right of approach* when it suspects a merchant vessel flying a foreign flag is actually of its own nationality and is concealing it to avoid investigation. Ordinarily merchant ships on the high seas are subject to control only by warships of their own nation in peacetime. But a warship may board a merchant vessel flying any flag for the specific purpose of verifying its nationality if it has reason to suspect it is of its own flag state.

5. A reciprocal treaty may grant the signatories authority to arrest each other's merchant vessels under specified circumstances. Such circumstances are usually in relation to such things as mutually-agreed-upon areas declared off limits to fishing boats for conservation purposes, the protection of submarine cables, or the suppression of slave trade. This authority extends only to arrest, and not to prosecution. The offenders must be turned over to the flag state for trial.

6. If a warship suspects a merchant vessel on the high seas of piracy, it may board her for investigation regardless of nationality and may arrest the crew if its suspicions prove justified. The crime of piracy is unique in that any nation may not only arrest but also *try* a pirate under its own municipal law, regardless of his nationali-

ty. The Convention on the High Seas defines piracy as "any illegal acts of violence, detention or any act of depredation, committed for private ends by the crew or passengers of a private ship or a private aircraft, and directed . . . against another ship or aircraft, or against persons or property on board such ship or aircraft." In order to classify as piracy, the acts must take place either on the high seas or "in a place outside the jurisdiction of any state." This last provision would cover air piracy over international waters or in outer space.

7. During war a warship may seize enemy merchant ships and, under some circumstances, neutral ships trading with the enemy.

Chapter VIII

AVIATION AND OUTER SPACE

Between the first airplane flight at Kitty Hawk, North Carolina, on December 17, 1903, and the outbreak of World War I in 1914, there was some international discussion about the legal status of airspace above nations, but it hardly seemed to most nations an urgent enough problem to require detailed study. With the outbreak of World War I it quite suddenly became a high-priority matter, though. In order to prevent aircraft dogfights from taking place over their territories, neutral nations in rapid order began to announce their claims to absolute sovereignty over their airspace, unlimited by any right of innocent passage.

These claims have never been disputed by other nations for the simple reason that all nations wanted the same right. Complete sovereignty over the airspace above nations has therefore become one of the rules of customary law that has 100 percent acceptance among the nations of the world. As an extension of the principle of the freedom of the high seas, the rule is that the aircraft of all nations have freedom of flight over international waters, but that freedom of flight ends unequivocally at the outer territorial limits of foreign nations. This differs from the law of the sea in that ships have certain rights of innocent passage through territorial waters and contiguous zones, but there are absolutely no exceptions insofar as aircraft are concerned.

It is a serious enough breach of international law for one nation to violate another's airspace that violation by military aircraft, and deliberate violation by civil aircraft for other than emergency reasons or the seeking of asylum, entitles the violated nation to shoot down the trespasser. In May, 1960, a U-2 observation plane piloted by a United States civilian named Francis Gary Powers was shot down over the Soviet Union. Because the aircraft had been taking reconnaissance photographs for the use of U.S. Army intelligence, the United States not only had no grounds for protest but received a strong protest from the Soviet Union. The Soviet Union also canceled a summit meeting scheduled between Nikita Khrushchev and President Dwight Eisenhower because of the violation.

When a violation of airspace by a nonmilitary plane is accidental, there is no right to fire on it. The violated nation may arrest it, however, and order it to land. The usual procedure is for military planes to force it to land, but after an examination of the crew and passengers, it is usually allowed to take off again under escort of military aircraft and is escorted out of the country. Sometimes a passenger plane that is obviously off course by accident is not even ordered to land, but is merely instructed by radio to fly in a holding pattern until military aircraft can get into the air and escort it to authorized territory. In 1973 Israel was censured by the U.N. General Assembly for shooting down an unarmed passenger plane that ignored its orders to land.

The United States is party to a number of conventions concerning civil aviation, including the 1970 Hague Convention for the Suppression of Hijacking. But the treaties that permit the passage of its aircraft over foreign nations and the use of foreign airports by them are all bilateral. This is true of all nations that offer international passenger and freight service. A separate treaty must be signed with each nation to which regular service is contemplated.

Much of the international law governing aircraft is modeled on the law of the sea. For example, aircraft are registered in the same manner as ships and may not be registered under more than one flag. However, because most airlines are either owned or subsidized by governments, the problem of flags of convenience for aircraft has never arisen. For instance, there are no American commercial aircraft registered in other nations except a few independently owned charter planes.

The law of outer space, despite being such a recent development, is quite definite on a number of points. One is that sovereign rights do not extend to outer space.

The first artificial satellite went into orbit about the earth on October 4, 1957. Since then, many others have been launched, but no nation has ever protested a violation of its airspace because of the passage of these satellites over its territory. This tacit acceptance by itself would make it a rule of customary law that such passage is permissible, but the U.N. General Assembly has reinforced the rule by passing a resolution specifically stating that the sovereignty of nations does not extend to that portion of outer space above them. The resolution did not define just where airspace ends and outer space begins, but that presents no problem at the moment because the minimum distance above the earth at which a satellite may be retained in orbit is far above the atmosphere, and airspace certainly cannot extend beyond the atmosphere because aircraft cannot fly where there is no air.

The law of outer space is so new that most of its rules are contained in three documents. Two are resolutions passed by the U.N. General Assembly in 1963. Since both were passed unanimously, they can be considered binding on all members of the United Nations.

The first resolution called upon all nations to "refrain from placing into orbit around the earth any objects carrying nuclear weapons or any other kinds of weapons of mass destruction, installing such weapons on celestial bodies, or stationing such weapons in outer space in any other manner." The second resolution reaffirmed some already existing rules, including the one denying any national sovereignty in outer space, and further stated these rules, among others:

1. The exploration and use of outer space is to be carried on for the benefit of all mankind.

2. Outer space is free for exploration and use by all nations equally.

3. Outer space and celestial bodies are not subject to territorial claim. (Both the Soviet Union and United States have specifically renounced any claims to sovereignty over the moon as the result of manned and unmanned moon landings in order to reinforce this principle.)

The third document is the Treaty on Principles Governing the Activities of States in the Exploration and Use of Outer Space, signed at Washington, D.C., on January 27, 1967. Although so far only the Soviet Union and the United States, both signatory to the treaty, have sent astronauts into outer space, sixty-five other nations have also ratified or acceded to it.

To some extent the treaty merely confirms the principles laid down in General Assembly resolutions, but these rules were new:

1. Nations must publicly disclose information about their activities in outer space.

2. Studies and exploration in outer space are to be conducted in such manner as to avoid contamination or adverse changes in the environment of the earth from the introduction of extraterrestrial matter.

3. The moon and other celestial bodies are to be used exclusively for peaceful purposes. The establishment of military bases, the testing of weapons, or military maneuvers are forbidden.

International lawyers have pointed out a fine difference between item 3 above and the U.N. resolution concerning spacecraft in orbit about the earth. Item 3 flatly prohibits military use of any sort, whereas the U.N. resolution merely prohibits weapons. The inference is that satellites in earth orbit may be used for military purposes not involivng weapons, such as reconnaissance.

In the past a major obstacle to disarmament treaties has been suspicion that one side or the other might secretly rearm. The solution to that problem is an efficent inspection system. The Soviet Union has always made that difficult, however, by refusing inspection teams open access to all parts of its territory. An advantage, from the U.S. point of view, of satellites equipped to take aerial photographs is that they provide a means for such inspection.

During the negotiation leading to the Outer Space Treaty, the Soviet Union attempted to make the use of satellites for reconnaissance purposes illegal, but the United States refused. To do otherwise would have given unnecessary military advantage to the Soviet Union. As an open society the military strength of the United States, at least in approximate terms, is information available to anyone in the world. But the Soviet Union, through such devices as a controlled press and the refusal of unrestricted travel in its territory by foreigners, has successfully managed to keep its military strength, and particularly its developments in nuclear weapons, much more of a mystery.

Chapter IX

INDIVIDUALS UNDER INTERNATIONAL LAW

Under municipal law animals have no rights, but they do have benefits. That is, suit cannot be brought on behalf of an animal, although it may be brought on behalf of the human owner for injury done to the animal, but there are laws, such as those forbidding inhuman treatment, that protects animals.

Under international law individuals are in a similar status to animals under municipal law: they possess benefits rather than rights. Wrongs done to them by foreign nations are considered wrongs against the nations of which they are nationals, not wrongs against the individuals themselves. The theory is that the nation itself suffers injury when one of its nationals is harmed.

Individuals therefore have no access to international courts or arbitral tribunals. They sometimes *are* permitted to ask for relief in municipal courts when the claims are international in nature, as in the case of *The Paquete Habana and the Lola v. the United States*, cited in Chapter II. It should be understood, though, that this is not a right, but is dependent upon permission by the defendant nation. It should also be pointed out that the decision in that case did not assess damages against the United States (except for the minor ones of court costs and legal fees) but merely returned to the claimants the amount obtained from the sale of their boats and cargoes. The Supreme Court ruling was merely a legal opinion, not a judgment for damages.

When an individual is damaged by a foreign nation, his own nation has complete liberty to file a claim, refrain from filing one, ask merely for an apology, or demand monetary compensation and settle for any amount it chooses. Any compensation paid is paid to the claimant nation, which is under no duty to turn it over to the injured individual. In actual practice, though, damages are usually calculated on the basis of the loss suffered by the individual, not the injury to the claimant nation, and the money is almost always given to the injured person.

Sometimes, when there is damage both to an individual and to his nation, arbitrators will separately compute the amounts. It is understood that this is merely a mathematical device used to arrive at a total figure, however, and that the entire sum is to be paid to the claimant nation. An example is the I'm Alone Case, which stemmed from an incident in 1929 and was settled in 1935.

On March 20, 1929, the Canadian schooner *I'm Alone*, known by U.S. authorities to be a rum-runner, was hailed by the U.S. Coast Guard vessel *Wolcott* off the coast of Louisiana in the Gulf of Mexico. Although the *I'm Alone* was beyond the three-mile limit on the high seas, a treaty signed in 1924 between the United States and Great Britain permitted the seizure on the high seas of vessels of the British Empire suspected of smuggling liquor if they were "the distance of one hour's sailing from the coast of the United States." The *I'm Alone* was within that distance.

When the *I'm Alone* refused to heave to and headed for open sea, the *Wolcott* followed in hot pursuit, periodically firing on the fleeing rum-runner until her gun jammed. Still in hot pursuit, the *Wolcott* radioed for assistance. Two days after pursuit began, on March 22, and now two hundred miles at sea, the U.S. Coast Guard cutter *Dexter* joined the pursuit and eventually sank the *I'm Alone*. One crew member drowned, but the captain and the rest of the crew were saved.

The 1924 treaty between the United States and Great Britain provided for an arbitral commission in the event of claims under the treaty. Canada's claim for damages was referred to that commission.

The ruling of the commission was rather long, but essentially evolved on the point that hot pursuit had not been continuous because the ship that actually did the sinking had joined the chase long after it began. The sinking was found not to be justified, and compensation was declared due to Canada.

Because during the course of the inquiry it had come to light that although registered in Canada, the *I'm Alone* had been owned by American citizens, no award was made to the Canadian Government in compensation for the loss of the ship. An amount of $25,666.50 was awarded for damages to the captain and the crew, however, who were Canadian citizens. An additional $25,000 was awarded for the insult to the Canadian Government for firing upon a ship on the high seas flying its flag. Although these amounts were listed separately, the total of $50,666.50 was all due to the Canadian Government.

As it happened the Canadian Government turned over to the captain and his crew the $25,666.50 awarded on their behalf, but it was under no obligation to do so.

As has been mentioned, a European Convention on Human Rights was signed in 1950 which guaranteed certain rights to the nationals of the signatory nations, among them humane treatment. However, there is no enforcement procedure for this convention, and could not be under international law, because that would involve interference in the internal affairs of nations.

As a result nations are free to treat their own nationals pretty much as they please. A nation is free to operate under any economic and political form it wishes to, ranging from socialism to capitalism and from absolute dictatorship to democracy. Even if it dissolves into anarchy and has no government at all, it is not in violation of international law. And its internal affairs, including its treatment of its nationals, are not subject to the rules of international law.

While nations have virtually unrestricted freedom to treat their own nationals as they please, customary law has set certain minimum international standards for the treatment of aliens. Nations have no obligation to admit aliens to their territories, but if they do, they are obliged to treat them in a civilized manner.

Vistiors or alien residents of a foreign nation, except
for persons enjoying diplomatic immunity, are subject to
the laws of that nation. Many American travelers, particularly young people in the drug-oriented subculture,
have belatedly discovered this to their sorrow. It is estimated by the State Department that somewhere around
eight hundred young Americans are in foreign prisons,
some of them serving sentences as long as twenty years.
And some of these sentences are merely on marijuana-
possession convictions that would have been only misde-
meanors in their home states.

One of the functions of American consuls is to assist
U.S. citizens to obtain their rights when arrested in foreign countries. But it should be understood that these
are rights under the laws of the foreign nation, not under the U.S. Constitution. An American consul will visit
you in jail if you are arrested in Turkey, and will arrange for you to get legal assistance, but he will have no
magic formula to get you out simply because you are an
American citizen. The "Constitutional rights" that protect
you in the event of arrest within the United States do
not extend to foreign courts.

The rights and duties of aliens are never precisely the
same as those of nationals, of course. A single standard
for both would simultaneously grant aliens rights no nation would be willing to give, and lose them all protection of their own native citizenship. They would be entitled to vote, draw welfare benefits, and freely enter any
trade or profession that some nations now bar to aliens.
But on the other hand they might be subject to treatment below minimum international standards, such as
torture, if the nation concerned used such practices on
its own nationals.

Minimum international standards for the treatment of
aliens came about during the nineteenth and early twentieth centuries, largely upon the insistence of the United
States and the Western European powers. In general
minimum standards bar such things as imprisonment
without trial, torture or other physical mistreatment,
looting or damage to property owned by aliens, unneces-

sarily long detention before trial, and severe punishment for trivial offenses.

During the period these standards were developing into customary law, they were resisted by many Latin American countries, which insisted that their municipal law applied equally to their nationals and to aliens. The United States was largely responsible for the eventual acceptance of minimum standards in those areas by exercising both diplomatic and economic pressure and, in some cases, sending in marines to enforce proper treatment of its citizens. Similar resistance by some of the small nations of Africa, the Middle East, and the Far East was met in like fashion by Great Britain and the nations of Western Europe.

With the U.N. General Assembly offering a forum in which protest by one nation against another can focus worldwide attention, modern nations tend to try to avoid arousing protest. The deliberate mistreatment of aliens has therefore become the exception rather than the rule in most areas of the world. In recent years the *people* of some small nations have shown strong resentment of what they regard as American economic imperialism by stoning American embassies and mistreating American visitors, but this does not necessarily reflect the official government policy of those nations. Actually, because many of these nations are the recipients of U.S. foreign aid, they tend to be rather careful in their treatment of Americans, not so much in observance of international law, but at least partly in recognition of the prestige and power of the United States.

A nation has the right to deport an alien at any time it chooses to. This was not always so. In the famous Boffolo Case of 1903 the Italian-Venezuelan Mixed Claims Commission held that the expulsion of Italian national Gennaro Boffolo from Venezuela was illegal because the government had given insufficient reason for the deportation. Custom has long since overturned this as a rule of international law, though. Nations now universally claim the right to expel aliens on no more specific grounds than the public good, and they are the sole arbiters of what constitutes the public good. Usually a reason is stated, but it is not required. And no matter how trivial the stated reason, it now appears that the deportee has no grounds for protest. In 1969, for example, a woman lecturer from England was deported from Malawi in East Africa for appearing at a party in a miniskirt.

As in all claims for damages done to individuals, the alien's government, not the alien himself, must bring an international claim in his behalf. In the interest of preserving friendly relations between nations, though, the rule of customary law is that the injured person must first exhaust the remedies offered by the courts of the defendant nation before his nation can bring an international claim. This is because a claim for damages on an international level usually involves an accusation of breaking international law, and this is a serious charge against another nation. However, when friendly relations have already been disrupted between the two nations by the nature of the dispute—if there has been repeated and continuous violation of aliens' rights, for instance, without proper redress by the local courts—this rule does not apply. The assumption in such instances is that the claimant nation's honor has been affronted, and therefore an international claim is justified without any preliminary legal maneuvers.

Except in such exceptional circumstances, the rule that local remedies must first be exhausted is applied rather strictly. A prime example is the Interhandel Case of 1959.

During World War II the United States seized the multimillion-dollar General Aniline and Film Corporation on the grounds that it was enemy-owned because it had a connection with the German I. G. Farben Company. Actually, although it did have such a connection, General Aniline and Film was Swiss-owned, and Switzerland was a neutral nation.

After World War II the Swiss firm started action to recover in the American courts. After nine years of litigation had apparently reached a dead end, in 1959 Switzerland started proceedings against the United States on behalf of the Swiss company in the International Court of Justice. But while the Interhandel Case was still pending before the Court, the U.S. Supreme Court ordered a new trial of the Swiss firm's action against U.S. authorities.

The ICJ dismissed Switzerland's claim on the grounds that local remedies had not been exhausted. In view of the long and unsuccessful litigation that had already taken place in the American courts, obviously the rule is that local remedies must be *completely* exhausted.

CHARTER OF
THE UNITED NATIONS

Amendments to the U.N. Charter

Amendments to Articles 23, 27, and 61 of the U. N. Charter, adopted by the General Assembly on Dec. 17, 1963, came into force on Aug. 31, 1965. The amendment to Article 23 enlarged the membership of the Security Council from 11 to 15. The amended Article 27 provided that decisions of the Security Council on procedural matters shall be made by an affirmative vote of 9 members (formerly 7) and on all other matters by an affirmative vote of 9 members (formerly 7), including the concurring votes of the 5 permanent members of the Security Council. The amendment to Article 61 enlarged the membership of the Economic and Social Council from 18 to 27.

An amendment to Article 109, adopted by the General Assembly on Dec. 20, 1965, came into force on June 12, 1968. The amendment provides that a General Conference of Member States for the purpose of reviewing the Charter may be held at a date and place to be fixed by a two-thirds vote of the members of the General Assembly and by a vote of any 9 members (formerly 7) of the Security Council.

CHARTER OF THE UNITED NATIONS

WE the peoples of the United Nations determined to save succeeding generations from the scourge of war, which twice in our lifetime has brought untold sorrow to mankind, and

To reaffirm faith in fundamental human rights, in the dignity and worth of the human person, in the equal rights of men and women and of nations large and small and

To establish conditions under which justice and respect for the obligations arising from treaties and other sources of international law can be maintained, and

To promote social progress and better standards of life in larger freedom, and for these ends

To practice tolerance and live together in peace with one another as good neighbors, and

To unite our strength to maintain international peace and security, and

To insure, by the acceptance of principles and the institution of methods, that armed force shall not be used, save in the common interest, and

To employ international machinery for the promotion of the economic and social advancement of all peoples, have resolved to combine our efforts to accomplish these aims.

Accordingly, our respective Governments, through representatives assembled in the city of San Francisco, who have exhibited their full powers found to be in good and due form, have agreed to the present Charter of the United Nations and do hereby establish an international organization to be known as the United Nations.

CHAPTER I

PURPOSES AND PRINCIPLES

Article 1

The purposes of the United Nations are:

1. To maintain international peace and security, and to that end: to take effective collective measures for the prevention and removal of threats to the peace, and for the suppression of acts of aggression or other breaches of the peace, and to bring about by peaceful means, and in conformity with the principles of justice and international law, adjustment or settlement of international disputes or situations which might lead to a breach of the peace;

2. To develop friendly relations among nations based on respect for the principle of equal rights and self-determination of

peoples, and to take other appropriate measures to strengthen universal peace;

3. To achieve international cooperation in solving international problems of an economic, social, cultural, or humanitarian character, and in promoting and encouraging respect for human rights and for fundamental freedoms for all without distinction as to race, sex, language, or religion; and

4. To be a center for harmonizing the actions of nations in the attainment of these common ends.

Article 2

The Organization and its Members in pursuit of the Purposes stated in Article 1, shall act in accordance with the following Principles:

1. The Organization is based on the principle of the sovereign equality of all its Members.

2. All Members, in order to ensure to all of them the rights and benefits resulting from membership, shall fulfill in good faith the obligations assumed by them in accordance with the present Charter.

3. All Members shall settle their international disputes by peaceful means in such a manner that international peace and security, and justice, are not endangered.

4. All Members shall refrain in their international relations from the threat or use of force against the territorial integrity or political independence of any state, or in any other manner inconsistent with the Purposes of the United Nations.

5. All Members shall give the United Nations every assistance in any action it takes in accordance with the present Charter, and shall refrain from giving assistance to any state against which the United Nations is taking preventive or enforcement action.

6. The Organization shall ensure that states which are not Members of the United Nations act in accordance with these Principles so far as may be necessary for the maintenance of international peace and security.

7. Nothing contained in the present Charter shall authorize the United Nations to intervene in matters which are essentially within the domestic jurisdiction of any state or shall require the Members to submit such matters to settlement under the present Charter; but this principle shall not prejudice the application of enforcement measures under Chapter VII.

CHAPTER II

MEMBERSHIP

Article 3

The original Members of the United Nations shall be the states which, having participated in the United Nations Conference on International Organization at San Francisco, or having previously signed the Declaration by United Nations of January 1, 1942, sign the present Charter and ratify it in accordance with Article 110.

Article 4

1. Membership in the United Nations is open to all other peace-loving states which accept the obligations contained in the present Charter and, in the judgment of the Organization, are able and willing to carry out these obligations.

2. The admission of any such state to membership in the United Nations will be effected by a decision of the General Assembly upon the recommendation of the Security Council.

Article 5

A Member of the United Nations against which preventive or enforcement action has been taken by the Security Council may be suspended from the exercise of the rights and privileges of membership by the General Assembly upon the recommendation of the Security Council. The exercise of these rights and privileges may be restored by the Security Council.

Article 6

A Member of the United Nations which has persistently violated the Principles contained in the present Charter may be expelled from the Organization by the General Assembly upon the recommendation of the Security Council.

CHAPTER III

ORGANS

Article 7

1. There are established as the principal organs of the United Nations; a General Assembly, a Security Council, an Economic and Social Council, a Trusteeship Council, an International Court of Justice, and a Secretariat.

2. Such subsidiary organs as may be found necessary may be established in accordance with the present Charter.

Article 8

The United Nations shall place no restrictions on the eligibility of men and women to participate in any capacity and under conditions of equality in its principal and subsidiary organs.

CHAPTER IV

THE GENERAL ASSEMBLY
Composition

Article 9

1. The General Assembly shall consist of all the members of the United Nations.

2. Each Member shall have not more than five representatives in the General Assembly.

Functions and Powers

Article 10

The General Assembly may discuss any questions or any matters within the scope of the present Charter or relating to the powers and functions of any organs provided for in the present Charter, and, except as provided in Article 12, may make recommendations to the Members of the United Nations or to the Security Council or to both on any such questions or matters.

Article 11

1. The General Assembly may consider the general principles of cooperation in the maintenance of international peace and security, including the principles governing disarmament and the regulation of armaments, and may make recommendations with regard to such principles to the Members or to the Security Council or to both.

2. The General Assembly may discuss any questions relating to the maintenance of international peace and security brought before it by any Member of the United Nations, or by the Security Council, or by a state which is not a Member of the United Nations, in accordance with Article 35, paragraph 2, and, except as provided in Article 12, may make recommendations with regard to any such question to the state or states concerned or to the Security Council or to both. Any such question on which action is necessary shall be referred to the

Security Council by the General Assembly either before or after discussion.

3. The General Assembly may call the attention of the Security Council to situations which are likely to endanger international peace and security.

4. The powers of the General Assembly set forth in this Article shall not limit the general scope of Article 10.

Article 12

1. While the Security Council is exercising in respect of any dispute or situation the functions assigned to it in the present Charter, the General Assembly shall not make any recommendations with regard to that dispute or situation unless the Security Council so requests.

2. The Secretary-General, with the consent of the Security Council, shall notify the General Assembly at each session of any matters relative to the maintenance of international peace and security which are being dealt with by the Security Council and shall similarly notify the General Assembly, or the Members of the United Nations if the General Assembly is not in session, immediately the Security Council ceases to deal with such matters.

Articles 13

1. The General Assembly shall initiate studies and make recommendations for the purpose of:

(a) promoting international cooperation in the political field and encouraging the progressive development of international law and its codification;

(b) promoting international cooperation in the economic, social, cultural, educational, and health fields, and assisting in the realization of human rights and fundamental freedoms for all without distinction as to race, sex, language, or religion.

2. The further responsibilities, functions and powers of the General Assembly with respect to matters mentioned in paragraph 1 (b) above are set forth in Chapters IX and X.

Article 14

Subject to the provisions of Article 12, the General Assembly may recommend measures for the peaceful adjustment of any situation, regardless of origin, which it deems likely to impair the general welfare or friendly relations among nations, including situations resulting from a violation of the provisions of the present Charter setting forth the Purposes and Principles of the United Nations.

Article 15

1. The General Assembly shall receive and consider annual and special reports from the Security Council; these reports shall include an account of the measures that the Security Council has decided upon or taken to maintain international peace and security.

2. The General Assembly shall receive and consider reports from the other organs of the United Nations.

Article 16

The General Assembly shall perform such functions with respect to the international trusteeship system as are assigned to it under Chapters XII and XIII, including the approval of the trusteeship agreements for areas not designated as strategic.

Article 17

1. The General Assembly shall consider and approve the budget of the Organization.

2. The expenses of the Organization shall be borne by the Members as apportioned by the General Assembly.

3. The General Assembly shall consider and approve any financial and budgetary arrangements with specialized agencies referred to in Article 57 and shall examine the administrative budgets of such specialized agencies with a view to making recommendations to the agencies concerned.

Voting

Article 18

1. Each member of the General Assembly shall have one vote.

2. Decisions of the General Assembly on important questions shall be made by a two-thirds majority of the members present and voting. These questions shall include: recommendations with respect to the maintenance of international peace and security, the election of the nonpermanent members of the Security Council, the election of the members of the Economic and Social Council, the election of members of the Trusteeship Council in accordance with paragraph 1 (c) of Article 86, the admission of new Members to the United Nations, the suspension of the rights and privileges of membership, the expulsion of Members, questions relating to the operation of the trusteeship system, and budgetary questions.

3. Decisions on other questions, including the determination of additional categories of questions to be decided by a two-thirds majority, shall be made by a majority of the members present and voting.

Article 19

A Member of the United Nations which is in arrears in the payment of its financial contributions to the Organization shall have no vote in the General Assembly if the amount of its arrears equals or exceeds the amount of the contributions due from it for the preceding two full years. The General Assembly may, nevertheless, permit such a Member to vote if it is satisfied that the failure to pay is due to conditions beyond the control of the Member.

Procedure
Article 20

The General Assembly shall meet in regular annual sessions and in such special sessions as occasion may require. Special sessions shall be convoked by the Secretary-General at the request of the Security Council or of a majority of the Members of the United Nations.

Article 21

The General Assembly shall adopt its own rules of procedure. It shall elect its President for each session.

Article 22

The General Assembly may establish such subsidiary organs as it deems necessary for the performance of its functions.

CHAPTER V

THE SECURITY COUNCIL
Composition

Article 23*

1. The Security Council shall consist of fifteen Members of the United Nations. The Republic of China, France, the Union of Soviet Socialist Republics, the United Kingdom of Great Britain and Northern Ireland, and the United States of America shall be permanent members of the Security Council. The General Assembly shall elect ten other Members of the United Nations to be non-permanent members of the Security Council, due regard being specially paid, in the first instance to the contribution of Members of the United Nations to the maintenance of international peace and security and to the other pur-

* As amended in 1965. See page 166.

poses of the Organization, and also to equitable geographical distribution.

2. The non-permanent members of the Security Council shall be elected for a term of two years. In the first election of the non-permanent members after the increase of the membership of the Security Council from eleven to fifteen, two of the four additional members shall be chosen for a term of one year. A retiring member shall not be eligible for immediate re-election.

3. Each member of the Security Council shall have one representative.

Functions and Powers

Article 24

1. In order to insure prompt and effective action by the United Nations, its Members confer on the Security Council primary responsibility for the maintenance of international peace and security, and agree that in carrying out its duties under this responsibility the Security Council acts on their behalf.

2. In discharging these duties the Security Council shall act in accordance with the Purposes and Principles of the United Nations. The specific powers granted to the Security Council for the discharge of these duties are laid down in Chapters VI, VII, VIII, and XII.

3. The Security Council shall submit annual and, when necessary, special reports to the General Assembly for its consideration.

Article 25

The Members of the United Nations agree to accept and carry out the decisions of the Security Council in accordance with the present Charter.

Article 26

In order to promote the establishment and maintenance of international peace and security with the least diversion for armaments of the world's human and economic resources, the Security Council shall be responsible for formulating, with the assistance of the Military Staff Committee referred to in Article 47, plans to be submitted to the Members of the United Nations for the establishment of a system for the regulation of armaments.

Voting

Article 27*

1. Each member of the Security Council shall have one vote.

2. Decisions of the Security Council on procedural matters shall be made by an affirmative vote of nine members.

3. Decisions of the Security Council on all other matters shall be made by an affirmative vote of nine members including the concurring votes of the permanent members; provided that, in decisions under Chapter VI, and under paragraph 3 of Article 52, a party to a dispute shall abstain from voting.

Procedure

Article 28

1. The Security Council shall be so organized as to be able to function continuously. Each member of the Security Council shall for this purpose be represented at all times at the seat of the Organization.

2. The Security Council shall hold periodic meetings at which each of its members may, if it so desires, be represented by a member of the government or by some other specially designated representative.

3. The Security Council may hold meetings at such places other than the seat of the Organization as in its judgment will best facilitate its work.

Article 29

The Security Council may establish such subsidiary organs as it deems necessary for the performance of its functions.

Article 30

The Security Council shall adopt its own rules of procedure, including the method of selecting its President.

Article 31

Any Member of the United Nations which is not a member of the Security Council may participate, without vote, in the discussion of any question brought before the Security Council whenever the latter considers that the interests of that Member are specially affected.

Article 32

Any Member of the United Nations which is not a member of the Security Council or any state which is not a Member of

* As amended in 1965. See page 166.

the United Nations, if it is a party to a dispute under considerations by the Security Council, shall be invited to participate, without vote, in the discussion relating to the dispute. The Security Council shall lay down such conditions as it deems just for the participation of a state which is not a Member of the United Nations.

CHAPTER VI

PACIFIC SETTLEMENT OF DISPUTES

Article 33

1. The parties to any dispute, the continuance of which is likely to endanger the maintenance of international peace and security, shall, first of all, seek a solution by negotiation, enquiry, mediation, conciliation, arbitration, judicial settlement, resort to regional agencies or arrangements, or other peaceful means of their own choice.

2. The Security Council shall, when it deems necessary, call upon the parties to settle their dispute by such means.

Article 34

The Security Council may investigate any dispute, or any situation which might lead to international friction or give rise to a dispute, in order to determine whether the continuance of the dispute or situation is likely to endanger the maintenance of international peace and security.

Article 35

1. Any Member of the United Nations may bring any dispute, or any situation of the nature referred to in Article 34 to the attention of the Security Council or of the General Assembly.

2. A state which is not a Member of the United Nations may bring to the attention of the Security Council or of the General Assembly any dispute to which it is a party if it accepts in advance, for the purposes of the dispute, the obligations of pacific settlement provided in the present Charter.

3. The proceedings of the General Assembly in respect of matters brought to its attention under this Article will be subject to the provisions of Articles 11 and 12.

Article 36

1. The Security Council may, at any stage of a dispute of the nature referred to in Article 33 or of a situation of like nature, recommended appropriate procedures or methods of adjustment.

2. The Security Council should take into consideration any procedures for the settlement of the dispute which have already been adopted by the parties.

3. In making recommendations under this Article the Security Council should also take into consideration that legal disputes should as a general rule be referred by the parties to the International Court of Justice in accordance with the provisions of the Statute of the Court.

Article 37

1. Should the parties to a dispute of the nature referred to in Article 33 fail to settle it by the means indicated in that Article, they shall refer it to the Security Council.

2. If the Security Council deems that the continuance of the dispute is in fact likely to endanger the maintenance of international peace and security, it shall decide whether to take action under Article 36 or to recommend such terms of settlement as it may consider appropriate.

Article 38

Without prejudice to the provisions of Articles 33 to 37, the Security Council may, if all the parties to any dispute so request, make recommendations to the parties with a view to a pacific settlement of the dispute.

CHAPTER VII

ACTION WITH RESPECT TO THREATS TO THE PEACE, BREACHES OF THE PEACE, AND ACTS OF AGGRESSION

Article 39

The Security Council shall determine the existence of any threat to the peace, breach of the peace, or act of aggression and shall make recommendations, or decide what measures shall be taken in accordance with Articles 41 and 42, to maintain or restore international peace and security.

Article 40

In order to prevent an aggravation of the situation, the Security Council may, before making the recommendations or deciding upon the measures provided for in Article 39, call upon the parties concerned to comply with such provisional measures as it deems necessary or desirable. Such provisional measures shall be without prejudice to the rights, claims, or position of the parties concerned. The Security Council shall duly take account of failure to comply with such provisional measures.

Article 41

The Security Council may decide what measures not involving the use of armed force are to be employed to give effect to its decisions, and it may call upon the Members of the United Nations to apply such measures. These may include complete or partial interruption of economic relations and of rail, sea, air, postal, telegraphic, radio, and other means of communication, and the severance of diplomatic relations.

Article 42

Should the Security Council consider that measures provided for in Article 41 would be inadequate or have proved to be inadequate, it may take such action by air, sea, or land forces as may be necessary to maintain or restore international peace and security. Such action may include demonstrations, blockade, and other operations by air, sea, or land forces of Members of the United Nations.

Article 43

1. All Members of the United Nations, in order to contribute to the maintenance of international peace and security, undertake to make available to the Security Council, on its call and in accordance with a special agreement or agreements, armed forces, assistance, and facilities, including rights of passage, necessary for the purpose of maintaining international peace and security.

2. Such agreement or agreements shall govern the numbers and types of forces, their degree of readiness and general location, and the nature of the facilities and assistance to be provided.

3. The agreement or agreements shall be negotiated as soon as possible on the initiative of the Security Council. They shall be concluded between the Security Council and Members or between the Security Council and groups of Members and shall be subject to ratification by the signatory states in accordance with their respective constitutional processes.

Article 44

When the Security Council has decided to use force it shall, before calling upon a Member not represented on it to provide armed forces in fulfillment of the obligations assumed under Article 43, invite that Member, if the Member so desires, to participate in the decisions of the Security Council concerning the employment of contingents of that Member's armed forces.

Article 45

In order to enable the United Nations to take urgent military measures, Members shall hold immediately available national air-force contingents for combined international enforcement action. The strength and degree of readiness of these contingents and plans for their combined action shall be determined, within the limits laid down in the special agreement or agreements referred to in Article 43, by the Security Council with the assistance of the Military Staff Committee.

Article 46

Plans for the application of armed force shall be made by the Security Council with the assistance of the Military Staff Committee.

Article 47

1. There shall be established a Military Staff Committee to advise and assist the Security Council on all questions relating to the Security Council's military requirements for the maintenance of international peace and security, the employment and command of forces placed at its disposal, the regulation of armaments, and possible disarmament.

2. The Military Staff Committee shall consist of the Chiefs of Staff of the permanent members of the Security Council or their representatives. Any Member of the United Nations not permanently represented on the Committee shall be invited by the Committee to be associated with it when the efficient discharge of the Committee's responsibilities requires the participation of that Member in its work.

3. The Military Staff Committee shall be responsible under the Security Council for the strategic direction of any armed forces placed at the disposal of the Security Council. Questions relating to the command of such forces shall be worked out subsequently.

4. The Military Staff Committee, with the authorization of the Security Council and after consultation with appropriate regional agencies, may establish regional subcommittees.

Article 48

1. The action required to carry out the decisions of the Security Council for the maintenance of international peace and security shall be taken by all the Members of the United Nations or by some of them, as the Security Council may determine.

2. Such decisions shall be carried out by the Members of the United Nations directly and through their action in the appropriate international agencies of which they are members.

Article 49

The Members of the United Nations shall join in affording mutual assistance in carrying out the measures decided upon by the Security Council.

Article 50

If preventive or enforcement measures against any state are taken by the Security Council, any other state, whether a Member of the United Nations or not, which finds itself confronted with special economic problems arising from the carrying out of those measures shall have the right to consult the Security Council with regard to a solution of those problems.

Article 51

Nothing in the present Charter shall impair the inherent right of individual or collective self-defense if an armed attack occurs against a Member of the United Nations, until the Security Council has taken measures necessary to maintain international peace and security. Measures taken by Members in the exercise of this right of self-defense shall be immediately reported to the Security Council and shall not in any way affect the authority and responsibility of the Security Council under the present Charter to take at any time such action as it deems necessary in order to maintain or restore international peace and security.

CHAPTER VIII

REGIONAL ARRANGEMENTS

Article 52

1. Nothing in the present Charter precludes the existence of regional arrangements or agencies for dealing with such matters relating to the maintenance of international peace and security as are appropriate for regional action, provided that such arrangements or agencies and their activities are consistent with the Purposes and Principles of the United Nations.

2. The Members of the United Nations entering into such arrangements or constituting such agencies shall make every effort to achieve pacific settlement of local disputes through such regional arrangements or by such regional agencies before referring them to the Security Council.

3. The Security Council shall encourage the development of pacific settlement of local disputes through such regional arrangements or by such regional agencies either on the initiative

of the states concerned or by reference from the Security Council.

4. This Article in no way impairs the application of Articles 34 and 35.

Article 53

1. The Security Council shall, where appropriate, utilize such regional arrangements or agencies for enforcement action under its authority. But no enforcement action shall be taken under regional arrangements or by regional agencies without the authorization of the Security Council, with the exception of measures against any enemy state, as defined in paragraph 2 of this Article, provided for pursuant to Article 107 or in regional arrangements directed against renewal of aggressive policy on the part of any such state, until such time as the Organization may, on request of the Governments concerned, be charged with the responsibility for preventing further aggression by such a state.

2. The term enemy state as used in paragraph 1 of this Article applies to any state which during the Second World War has been an enemy of any signatory of the present Charter.

Article 54

The Security Council shall at all times be kept fully informed of activities undertaken or in contemplation under regional arrangements or by regional agencies for the maintenance of international peace and security.

CHAPTER IX

INTERNATIONAL ECONOMIC AND SOCIAL COOPERATION

Article 55

With a view to the creation of conditions of stability and well-being which are necessary for peaceful and friendly relations among nations based on respect for the principle of equal rights and self-determination of peoples, the United Nations shall promote:

(a) higher standards of living, full employment, and conditions of economic and social progress and development;

(b) solutions of international economic, social, health, and related problems; and international cultural and educational cooperation; and

(c) universal respect for, and observance of, human rights and fundamental freedoms for all without distinction as to race, sex, language, or religion.

Article 56

All Members pledge themselves to take joint and separate action in cooperation with the Organization for the achievement of the purposes set forth in Article 55.

Article 57

1. The various specialized agencies, established by intergovernmental agreement and having wide international responsibilities, as defined in their basic instruments, in economic, social, cultural, educational, health, and related fields, shall be brought into relationship with the United Nations in accordance with the provisions of Article 63.

2. Such agencies thus brought into relationship with the United Nations are hereinafter referred to as specialized agencies.

Article 58

The Organization shall make recommendations for the coordination of the policies and activities of the specialized agencies.

Article 59

The Orgainzation shall, where appropriate, initiate negotiations among the states concerned for the creation of any new specialized agencies required for the accomplishment of the purposes set forth in Article 55.

Article 60

Responsibility for the discharge of the functions of the Organization set forth in this Chapter shall be vested in the General Assembly and, under the authority of the General Assembly, in the Economic and Social Council, which shall have for this purpose the powers set forth in Chapter X.

CHAPTER X

ECONOMIC AND SOCIAL COUNCIL
Composition

Article 61*

1. The Economic and Social Council shall consist of twenty-seven Members of the United Nations elected by the General Assembly.

2. Subject to the provisions of paragraph 3, nine members of

* As amended in 1965. See page 166.

the Economic and Social Council shall be elected each year for a term of three years. A retiring member shall be eligible for immediate reelection.

3. At the firse election after the increase in the membership of the Economic and Social Council from eighteen to twenty-seven members, in addition to the members elected in place of the six members whose term of the office expires at the end of that year, nine additional members shall be elected. Of these nine additional members, the term of office of three members so elected shall expire at the end of one year, and of three other members at the end of two years, in accordance with arrangements made by the General Assembly.

4. Each member of the Economic and Social Council shall have one representative.

Functions and Powers

Article 62

1. The Economic and Social Council may make or initiate studies and reports with respect to international economic, social, cultural, educational, health, and related matters and may make recommendations with respect to any such matters to the General Assembly, to the Members of the United Nations, and to the specialized agencies concerned.

2. It may make recommendations for the purpose of promoting respect for, and observance of, human rights and fundamental freedoms for all.

3. It may prepare draft conventions for submission to the General Assembly with respect to matters falling within its competence.

4. It may call, in accordance with the rules prescribed by the United Nations, international conferences on matters falling within its competence.

Article 63

1. The Economic and Social Council may enter into agreements with any of the agencies referred to in Article 57, defining the terms on which the agency concerned shall be brought into relationship with the United Nations. Such agreements shall be subject to approval by the General Assembly.

2. It may coordinate the activities of the specialized agencies through consultation with and recommendations to such agencies and through recommendations to the General Assembly and to the Members of the United Nations.

Article 64

1. The Economic and Social Council may take appropriate steps to obtain regular reports from the specialized agencies. It

may make arrangements with the Members of the United Nations and with the specialized agencies to obtain reports on the steps taken to give effect to its own recommendations and to recommendations on matters falling within its competence made by the General Assembly.

2. It may communicate its observations on these reports to the General Assembly.

Article 65

The Economic and Social Council may furnish information to the Security Council and shall assist the Security Council upon its request.

Article 66

1. The Economic and Social Council shall perform such functions as fall within its competence in connection with the carrying out of the recommendations of the General Assembly.

2. It may, with the approval of the General Assembly, perform services at the request of Members of the United Nations and at the request of specialized agencies.

3. It shall perform such other functions as are specified elsewhere in the present Charter or as may be assigned to it by the General Assembly.

Voting

Article 67

1. Each member of the Economic and Social Council shall have one vote.

2. Decisions of the Economic and Social Council shall be made by a majority of the members present and voting.

Procedure

Article 68

The Economic and Social Council shall set up commissions in economic and social fields and for the promotion of human rights, and such other commissions as may be required for the performance of its functions.

Article 69

The Economic and Social Council shall invite any Member of the United Nations to participate, without vote, in its deliberations on any matter of particular concern to that Member.

Article 70

The Economic and Social Council may make arrangements for representatives of the specialized agencies to participate, without vote, in its deliberations and in those of the commissions established by it, and for its representatives to participate in the deliberations of the specialized agencies.

Article 71

The Economic and Social Council may make suitable arrangements for consultation with non-governmental organizations which are concerned with matters within its competence. Such arrangements may be made with international organizations and, where appropriate, with national organizations after consultation with the Member of the United Nations concerned.

Article 72

1. The Economic and Social Council shall adopt its own rules of procedure, including the method of selecting its President.

2. The Economic and Social Council shall meet as required in accordance with its rules, which shall include provision for the convening of meetings on the request of a majority of its members.

CHAPTER XI

DECLARATION REGARDING NON-SELF-GOVERNING TERRITORIES

Article 73

Members of the United Nations which have or assume responsibilities for the administration of territories whose peoples have not yet attained a full measure of self-government recognize the principle that the interests of the inhabitants of these territories are paramount, and accept as a sacred trust the obligation to promote to the utmost, within the system of international peace and security established by the present Charter, the well-being of the inhabitants of these territories, and, to this end:

(a) to ensure, with due respect for the culture of the peoples concerned, their political, economic, social, and educational advancement, their just treatment, and their protection against abuses;

(b) to develop self-government, to take due account of the political aspirations of the peoples, and to assist them in the progressive development of their free political institutions, according to the particular circumstances of each territory and its peoples and their varying stages of advancement;

(c) to further international peace and security;

(d) to promote constructive measures of development, to encourage research, and to cooperate with one another and, when and where appropriate, with specialized international bodies with a view to the practical achievement of the social, economic, and scientific purposes set forth in this Article; and

(e) to transmit regularly to the Secretary-General for information purposes, subject to such limitation as security and constitutional considerations may require, statistical and other information of a technical nature relating to economic, social, and educational conditions in the territories for which they are respectively responsible other than those territories to which Chapters XII and XIII apply.

Article 74

Members of the United Nations also agree that their policy in respect of the territories to which this Chapter applies, no less than in respect of their metropolitan areas, must be based on the general principle of good-neighborliness, due account being taken of the interests and well-being of the rest of the world, in social, economic, and commercial matters.

CHAPTER XII

INTERNATIONAL TRUSTEESHIP SYSTEM

Article 75

The United Nations shall establish under its authority an international trusteeship system for the administration and supervision of such territories as may be placed thereunder by subsequent individual agreements. These territories are hereinafter referred to as trust territories.

Article 76

The basic objectives of the trusteeship system, in accordance with the Purposes of the United Nations laid down in Article 1 of the present Charter, shall be:

(a) to further international peace and security;

(b) to promote the political, economic, social, and educational advancement of the inhabitants of the trust territories, and their progressive development towards self-government or independence as may be appropriate to the particular circumstances of each territory and its peoples and the freely expressed wishes of the peoples concerned, and as may be provided by the terms of each trusteeship agreement;

(c) to encourage respect for human rights and for fundamental freedoms for all without distinction as to race, sex, language, or religion, and to encourage recognition of the interdependence of the peoples of the world; and

(d) to ensure equal treatment in social, economic, and commercial matters for all Members of the United Nations and their nationals, and also equal treatment for the latter in the administration of justice, without prejudice to the attainment of the foregoing objectives and subject to the provisions of Article 80.

Article 77

1. The trusteeship system shall apply to such territories in the following categories as may be placed thereunder by means of trusteeship agreements:

(a) territories now held under mandate;

(b) territories which may be detached from enemy states as a result of the Second World War; and

(c) territories voluntarily placed under the system by states responsible for their administration.

2. It will be a matter for subsequent agreement as to which territories in the foregoing categories will be brought under the trusteeship system and upon what terms.

Article 78

The trusteeship system shall not apply to territories which have become Members of the United Nations, relationship among which shall be based on respect for the principle of sovereign equality.

Article 79

The terms of trusteeship for each territory to be placed under the trusteeship system, including any alteration or amendment, shall be agreed upon by the states directly concerned, including the mandatory power in the case of territories held under mandate by a Member of the United Nations, and shall be approved as provided for in Articles 83 and 85.

Article 80

1. Except as may be agreed upon in individual trusteeship agreements, made under Articles 77, 79, and 81, placing each territory under the trusteeship system, and until such agreements have been concluded, nothing in this Chapter shall be construed in or of itself to alter in any manner the rights whatsoever of any states or any peoples or the terms of existing international instruments to which Members of the United Nations may respectively be parties.

2. Paragraph 1 of this Article shall not be interpreted as giving grounds for delay or postponement of the negotiation and

conclusion of agreements for placing mandated and other territories under the trusteeship system as provided for in Article 77.

Article 81

The trusteeship agreement shall in each case include the terms under which the trust territory will be administered and designate the authority which will exercise the administration of the trust territory. Such authority, hereinafter called the administering authority, may be one or more states or the Orgainzation itself.

Article 82

There may be designated, in any trusteeship agreement, a strategic area or areas which may include part or all of the trust territory to which the agreement applies, without prejudice to any special agreement or agreements made under Article 43.

Article 83

1. All functions of the United Nations relating to strategic areas, including the approval of the terms of the trusteeship agreements and of their alteration or amendment, shall be exercised by the Security Council.

2. The basic objectives set forth in Article 76 shall be applicable to the people of each strategic area.

3. The Security Council shall, subject to the provisions of the trusteeship agreements and without prejudice to security considerations, avail itself of the assistance of the Trusteeship Council to perform those functions of the United Nations under the trusteeship system relating to political, economic, social, and educational matters in the strategic areas.

Article 84

It shall be the duty of the administering authority to ensure that the trust territory shall play its part in the maintenance of international peace and security. To this end the administering authority may make use of volunteer forces, facilities, and assistance from the trust territory in carrying out the obligations towards the Security Council undertaken in this regard by the administering authority, as well as for local defense and the maintenance of law and order within the trust territory.

Article 85

1. The functions of the United Nations with regard to trusteeship agreements for all areas not designated as strategic, including the approval of the terms of the trusteeship agreements

and of their alteration or amendment, shall be exercised by the General Assembly.

2. The Trusteeship Council, operating under the authority of the General Assembly, shall assist the General Assembly in carrying out these functions.

CHAPTER XIII

THE TRUSTEESHIP COUNCIL
Composition

Article 86

1. The Trusteeship Council shall consist of the following Members of the United Nations:

(a) those Members administering trust territories;

(b) such of those Members mentioned by name in Article 23 as are not administering trust territories; and

(c) as many other Members elected for three-year terms by the General Assembly as may be necessary to ensure that the total number of members of the Trusteeship Council is equally divided between those Members of the United Nations which administer trust territories and those which do not.

2. Each member of the Trusteeship Council shall designate one specially qualified person to represent it therein.

Functions and Powers

Article 87

The General Assembly and, under its authority, the Trusteeship Council, in carrying out their functions, may:

(a) consider reports submitted by the administering authority;

(b) accept petitions and examine them in consultation with the administering authority;

(c) provide for periodic visits to the respective trust territories at times agreed upon with the administering authority; and

(d) take these and other actions in conformity with the terms of the trusteeship agreements.

Article 88

The Trusteeship Council shall formulate a questionnaire on the political, economic, social, and educational advancement of the inhabitants of each trust territory, and the administering authority for each trust territory within the competence of the General Assembly shall make an annual report to the General Assembly upon the basis of such questionnaire.

Voting

Article 89

1. Each member of the Trusteeship Council shall have one vote.

2. Decisions of the Trusteeship Council shall be made by a majority of the members present and voting.

Procedure

Article 90

1. The Trusteeship Council shall adopt its own rules of procedure, including the method of selecting its President.

2. The Trusteeship Council shall meet as required in accordance with its rules, which shall include provision for the convening of meetings on the request of a majority of its members.

Article 91

The Trusteeship Council shall, when appropriate, avail itself of the assistance of the Economic and Social Council and of the specialized agencies in regard to matters with which they are respectively concerned.

CHAPTER XIV

THE INTERNATIONAL COURT OF JUSTICE

Article 92

The International Court of Justice shall be the principal judicial organ of the United Nations. It shall function in accordance with the annexed Statute, which is based upon the Statute of the Permanent Court of International Justice and forms an integral part of the present Charter.

Article 93

1. All Members of the United Nations are *ipso facto* parties to the Statute of the International Court of Justice.

2. A state which is not a Member of the United Nations may become a party to the Statute of the International Court of Justice on condition to be determined in each case by the General Assembly upon the recommendation of the Security Council.

Article 94

1. Each Member of the United Nations undertakes to comply with the decision of the International Court of Justice in any case to which it is a party.

2. If any party to a case fails to perform the obligations incumbent upon it under a judgment rendered by the Court, the other party may have recourse to the Security Council, which may, if it deems necessary, make recommendations or decide upon measures to be taken to give effect to the judgment.

Article 95

Nothing in the present Charter shall prevent Members of the United Nations from entrusting the solution of their differences to other tribunals by virtue of agreements already in existence or which may be concluded in the future.

Article 96

1. The General Assembly or the Security Council may request the International Court of Justice to give an advisory opinion on any legal question.

2. Other organs of the United Nations and specialized agencies, which may at any time be so authorized by the General Assembly, may also request advisory opinions of the Court on legal questions arising within the scope of their activities.

CHAPTER XV

THE SECRETARIAT

Article 97

The Secretariat shall comprise a Secretary-General and such staff as the Organization may require. The Secretary-General shall be appointed by the General Assembly upon the recommendation of the Security Council. He shall be the chief administrative officer of the Organization.

Article 98

The Secretary-General shall act in that capacity in all meetings of the General Assembly, of the Security Council, of the Economic and Social Council, and of the Trusteeship Council, and shall perform such other functions as are entrusted to him by these organs. The Secretary-General shall make an annual report to the General Assembly on the work of the Organization.

Article 99

The Secretary-General may bring to the attention of the Security Council any matter which in his opinion may threaten the maintenance of international peace and security.

Article 100

1. In the performance of their duties the Secretary-General and the staff shall not seek or receive instructions from any government or from any other authority external to the Organization. They shall refrain from any action which might reflect on their position as international officials responsible only to the Organization.

2. Each Member of the United Nations undertakes to respect the exclusively international character of the responsibilities of the Secretary-General and the staff and not to seek to influence them in the discharge of their responsibilities.

Article 101

1. The staff shall be appointed by the Secretary-General under regulations established by the General Assembly.

2. Appropriate staffs shall be permanently assigned to the Economic and Social Council, the Trusteeship Council, and, as required, to other organs of the United Nations. These staffs shall form a part of the Secretariat.

3. The paramount consideration in the employment of the staff and in the determination of the conditions of service shall be the necessity of securing the highest standards of efficiency, competence, and integrity. Due regard shall be paid to the importance of recruiting the staff on as wide a geographical basis as possible.

CHAPTER XVI

MISCELLANEOUS PROVISIONS

Article 102

1. Every treaty and every international agreement entered into by any Member of the United Nations after the present Charter comes into force shall as soon as possible be registered with the Secretariat and published by it.

2. No party to any such treaty or international agreement which has not been registered in accordance with the provisions of paragraph 1 of this Article may invoke that treaty or agreement before any organ of the United Nations.

Article 103

In the event of a conflict between the obligations of the Members of the United Nations under the present Charter and their obligations under any other international agreement, their obligations under the present Charter shall prevail.

Article 104

The Organization shall enjoy in the territory of each of its Members such legal capacity as may be necessary for the exercise of its functions and the fulfillment of its purposes.

Article 105

1. The Organization shall enjoy in the territory of each of its Members such privileges and immunities as are necessary for the fulfillment of its purposes.

2. Representatives of the Members of the United Nations and officials of the Organization shall similarly enjoy such privileges and immunities as are necessary for the independent exercise of their functions in connection with the Organization.

3. The General Assembly may make recommendations with a view to determining the details of the application of paragraphs 1 and 2 of this Article or may propose conventions to the Members of the United Nations for this purpose.

CHAPTER XVII

TRANSITIONAL SECURITY ARRANGEMENTS

Article 106

Pending the coming into force of such special agreements referred to in Article 43 as in the opinion of the Security Council enable it to begin the exercise of its responsibilities under Article 42, the parties to the Four-Nation Declaration, signed at Moscow, October 30, 1943, and France shall, in accordance with the provisions of paragraph 5 of that Declaration, consult with one another and, as occasion requires with other Members of the United Nations with a view to such joint action on behalf of the Organization as may be necessary for the purpose of maintaining international peace and security.

Article 107

Nothing in the present Charter shall invalidate or preclude action, in relation to any state which during the Second World War has been an enemy of any signatory to the present Charter, taken or authorized as a result of that war by the Governments having responsibility for such action.

CHAPTER XVIII

AMENDMENTS*

Article 108

Amendments to the present Charter shall come into force for all Members of the United Nations when they have been adopted by a vote of two thirds of the members of the General Assembly and ratified in accordance with their respective constitutional processes by two thirds of the Members of the United Nations, including all the permanent members of the Security Council.

Article 109†

1. A General Conference of the Members of the United Nations for the purpose of reviewing the present Charter may be held at a date and place to be fixed by a two-thirds vote of the members of the General Assembly and by a vote of any nine members of the Security Council. Each Member of the United Nations shall have one vote in the conference.

2. Any alteration of the present Charter recommended by a two-thirds vote of the conference shall take effect when ratified in accordance with their respective constitutional processes by two-thirds of the Members of the United Nations including all the permanent members of the Security Council.

3. If such a conference has not been held before the tenth annual session of the General Assembly following the coming into force of the present Charter, the proposal to call such a conference shall be placed on the agenda of that session of the General Assembly, and the conference shall be held if so decided by a majority vote of the members of the General Assembly and by a vote of any seven members of the Security Council.

CHAPTER XIX

RATIFICATION AND SIGNATURE

Article 110

1. The present Charter shall be ratified by the signatory states in accordance with their respective constitutional processes.

* For amendments enacted in 1965 and 1968, see page 166.
† As amended in 1968. See page 166.

2. The ratifications shall be deposited withe Government of the United States of America, which shall notify all the signatory states of each deposit as well as the Secretary-General of the Organization when he has been appointed.

3. The present Charter shall come into force upon the deposit of ratifications by the Republic of China, France, the Union of Soviet Socialist Republics, the United Kingdom of Great Britain and Northern Ireland, and the United States of America, and by a majority of the other signatory states. A protocol of the ratifications deposited shall thereupon be drawn up by the Government of the United States of America which shall communicate copies thereof to all the signatory states.

4. The states signatory to the present Charter which ratify it after it has come into force will become original Members of the United Nations on the date of the deposit of their respective ratifications.

Article 111

The present Charter, of which the Chinese, French, Russian, English, and Spanish texts are equally authentic, shall remain deposited in the archives of the Government of the United States of America. Duly certified copies thereof shall be transmitted by that Government to the Governments of the other signatory states.

IN FAITH WHEREOF the representatives of the Governments of the United Nations have signed the present Charter.

DONE at the city of San Francisco the twenty-sixth day of June, one thousand nine hundred and forty-five.

INDEX

www.ingramcontent.com/pod-product-compliance
Lightning Source LLC
Chambersburg PA
CBHW020202200326
41521CB00005BA/227